I NEVER SAW THE SUN RISE

I NEVER SAW THE SUN RISE

by
Joan Donlan

CompCare® Publishers
2415 Annapolis Lane
Minneapolis, Minnesota 55441

Published in the United States
by CompCare Publishers,

Library of Congress Catalog Card
No. 77-87738
ISBN No. 0-89638-007-6

Inquiries, orders, and catalog requests should be addressed to
CompCare Publishers
2415 Annapolis Lane
Minneapolis, MN 55441
Call toll free 800/328-3330
(Minnesota residents 612/559-4800)

Illustrations by the author.

10 11 12
88 89 90

Dedication

This book is for Jill,
the one who didn't come home.

Contents

Acknowledgments

I am grateful to the following:

Helen Dalton & Kay Cram
for having faith in me

Diane DuCharme
for her encouragement and help

Irene Whitney
for getting this off the ground

Tom Tietze
for his inspiration

Don Anderson
for waiting

The Staff at St. Mary's including:
Kevin, Gary, Keith, Jenny, Carol, Mike,
Mary, Celinda, Melissa, Jeff P.,
Jeff M., Elton, Jim, Pat (Mumbles), Ken R.
for teaching me how to live

Bob
for his hugs

Connie
for her sunshine

Kate
for her laughter

Mary
for her constant friendship

Buzz
for listening

My family
for their support

God
without whom this author would not be possible

Bill
for taking time

Gregg
for showing me God's love

Keith
for his prayers

Ivars
for his guidance

Pfeffer
for her love

Pat M.
for his gentleness

Norby
for his silence

Vic E.
for his care

Barb G.
for her understanding

Seiche
for his beautiful life

and my special friend,
Melanie . . . for just being there.

Cast of characters

Hubert
A Spring Valley rookie cop

Sadie
My slightly crazy friend from Spring Valley

Suki Foster "Cherries"
Well-endowed friend from Spring Valley

Brendan
Neat cop-friend from Spring Valley

Det. Reddy
Detective for Clairdale

Soani
Witch name for myself

Roy Wilhelm
Cop-friend from Willowood

Simon
Stompin' grounds buddy from Spring Valley

"Fries"
Friend from school and stable

Trella Lexie
Horse friend

Lou Harris
Happy over-active friend from Virginia

"Stash" Hannan
Junkie from school

Denny LaVerse
Race car driver, met him when he picked me up hitchhiking

Rico Michelson
Alcoholic boy friend from school

Kevin Adams
Christian cop from Willowood . . . good friend

Lisa Adams
Kevin's wife

Joy Adams
Kevin and Lisa's youngest daughter

"Siren"
Extremely rowdy friend from Spring Valley

Dan and Preston
Boy friends that belonged to somebody in Spring Valley

Neil
Junkie friend from the bowling alley in Spring Valley

Brent Wiser
Counselor from Christian youth organization

Ray
Junkie friend of "Stash" Hannan

Margo
Ray's girl friend

Luke
Christian friend from the Work Crew at One Way camp

Spaceman
Pusher, since turned Christian and straight

Joella Heathers
Friend who died suddenly in eighth grade of encephalitis

Det. Lucas Rogers
Detective from a nearby town

Dan Hale
Boy friend through most of tenth grade . . . since gone straight

Shelly
Baudy waitress from a local sandwich shoppe

Zombie
Burnt-out girl from school

Artful Dodger
A junkie friend of Dan's and mine, also my brother's good friend — now straight

Mrs. Williams
Algebra teacher in ninth grade

Dean
Very vague kind of helper from Spring Valley; he gave me his number on a cigarette box

Fred Contoree
Junkie friend — Dan's, Dodger's, my brother's, and mine; since gone straight and is now married

Bill
Counselor from treatment; frequently gave the parents' lectures

Rodney
Kid from treatment, real comedian

Tim and Nic
Junkie Foosball freaks from school

Terry
Junkie friend and pusher from school, since gone straight

Miss Cambridge
Health teacher and basketball coach — neat person

"Vanilla Piles" and "Saucy"
Hall monitors at school

S'lins
Sophisticated friend from Spring Valley

Brett Green
Scandal-seeking girl friend from Spring Valley

Cris
Christian counselor from the One Way camp, involved in deliverence

Chase
Junkie friend of my brother's that died

Pastor Lavin
Pastor friend of Cris', also involved in deliverance

Ed DeForest
Well-known expert on demonology, friend of Pastor Lavin and Cris

Carrie
Daughter of a Spring Valley cop, waitress at the bowling alley

Ed
Spring Valley member of the Police Reserve, also a snow-plow driver

Dr. Wesley
Psychologist involved with getting me into treatment

Dr. Donovan
Psychiatrist that Wesley worked with, also helped with the above

Eric
Manager at the Willowood Country Kitchen

Mitchel
Also known as "Turd", Foosball king of the bowling alley

Barb
Counselor in Detox, taught me how to feel like a kid sometimes

Robert
Counselor in Detox, I was always wary of him . . . he was so right on

Debb
Counselor in Detox, neat lady, made a good temporary "Mom"

Andy
Counselor in Detox, fantastic hugs

Erik
Also known as "Mumbles," Detox counselor, Foosball champ

Lauren
Junkie that got sent to another treatment center for sniffing aerosal

Lucy, Robin
Two girls from Detox, Robin was my first roomate

Charley
Hard-ass kid from Detox, called "Casa Nova" by the cleaning lady

Farlin
Very immature Cherokee imp, Donny Osmund fan, also from Detox

Ed Cortine
Kid from Detox, spacey, quiet, spoke in a monotone

Cindi
Good friend, came to Detox after several group homes

Peter
Extremely prejudiced, sent to Detox for addiction to sniffing gasoline

Jonny B.
Heroin addict in Detox, has since been counseling in chemical dependency

George
Junkie in Detox that got high and got arrested

Liza
Boy-loving junkie from Detox, got kicked out or split — I can't remember

Dr. Gilbertson
My doctor through treatment

Adam
Tall, jiving kid from Detox, split treatment on his own accord

Paula
Long-haired girl from Indonesia, met in Detox

Anne
Beautiful Indian girl, my roommate in Detox, before I went into treatment

Kathy
Sleazy girl from Detox, attended Willowood High School

Linda
Counselor from treatment, gentle, soft-spoken

Joseph
Counselor from treatment for the other squad

Ruby
Super neat girl, my roommate for most of treatment

Kitty
My old babysitter, has now gone into nursing

Chris Bains
Dan's girl friend while I was in Detox, has since married Fred C.

Carl
Gentle hospital chaplain, did lectures on grief in treatment

Joel
Counselor for Outpatient, really good guy, since gone to medical school

Sue
Friend that I met after treatment, just gone straight, had a great laugh

Jerry Martin
Guy from halfway house, ex-resident that killed himself

Mark
Boy friend after treatment, met over CB radio

Order of events

Aug. 8	"Deliverance" at One Way Camp.
Aug. 27	Met Officer Roy Wilhelm, Willowood.
Aug. 30	Orientation Willowood High School. Start tenth grade.
Sept. 5	Went out with Rico and Stash.
Sept. 6	Willowood football game.
Sept. 8	Sadie's lake party.
Sept. 13	Football game with Stash. Exorcism.
Sept. 14	Kidnapping, Cris.
Sept. 19	Seiche colic from green hay. Called vet. Colt cast in stall.
Sept. 20	Rode Seiche in Homecoming Parade at Willowood.
Sept. 28	One Way house. "Deliverance."
Oct. 1	Busted for suspected possession. Clairdale. Lou to jail. Neil to J.C. [juvenile center].
Oct. 3	Willowood City Hall, court. Lou given a year probation.
Oct. 4	Clairdale Homecoming.
Oct. 6	Kevin's baby born.
Oct. 14	Dinner with Roy. Spatts [Sadie's horse] may have a broken leg. One Way. "Deliverance."
Oct. 28	Saw Simon standing in the rain.
Oct. 31	Hallowe'en. Rode Seiche around neighborhood after dark, with big reflectors on his buns.
Nov. 12	Speed.
Nov. 13	Decided I am insane. Love drugs.
Nov. 17	Housed Ray and Margo in our tree fort. [They were running away.]
Nov. 25	Party.
Nov. 26	Hauled hay to put in loft. Met Simon at Pizza Place.
Dec. 13	To One Way. Dan over.
Dec. 21	Dan, Pastor and Cris at One Way house. "Deliverance."
Dec. 25	Christmas.
Dec. 26	Thirty hits of zip.

Dec. 28	Confrontation with parents about school.
Dec. 31	Acid. Walking around Willowood.
Jan. 1	Acid. Sadie sprains ankle.
Jan. 5	Dan is in S. America with his family.
Jan. 8	One Way. Close to suicide from anticipation.
Jan. 12	Dan home. Brought me a ring.
Jan. 15	Acid.
Jan. 16	Talk of St. Vincent's.
Jan. 17	Artful Dodger to St. Vincent's Detox.
Jan. 18	Acid.
Jan. 19	Acid.
Jan. 20	Bought a bag, drank wine, toked seven bowls.
Jan. 28	Eight in the morning, appointment at St. Vincent's.
Jan. 29	Leave for St. Vincent's hospital.
Jan. 30	Moved into Detox.
Feb. 27	First night in Treatment.
Mar. 4	Artful Dodger goes home from Treatment.
Mar. 21	Dan comes into Treatment.
Mar. 27	"Last Supper."
Apr. 3	Home from Treatment.
Apr. 13	Happy sweet sixteen.
June 24	Off to camp.
June 28	Christian youth camp.
Sept. 23	Jerry Martin's funeral.
Sept. 28	Car accident.
Oct. 17	"Silas" [old abandoned house] burns.
Dec. 11	Home from hospital [after hitting head in cooler working as waitress at Country Kitchen].
Jan. 29	Rode Seiche to new home.
Jan. 30	I have been straight for one year today.

Editor's note: This manuscript, which represents a year and a half of a teenager's diary-notebook, has been printed just as it came to us. Only the names of people (including her own) and places have been changed. Any minor additions for purposes of clarity are shown in brackets. We have not corrected the occasional misspellings. Nor have we altered the "street talk," as she calls it, the tough language that may offend older generations but which has become part of today's youth jargon. Chemical dependency is an angry disease. This author, who is a quiet, middle-America teenager, showed this anger — along with her self-destroying dislike of herself — only in her writing. Since her story is very real, we want her to tell it in her own words — as it happened. She selected "Joan Donlan" as her pen name. This is a purely fictional name, and the relationship of the author to anyone else of the same name is coincidental.

Please read this first . . .

My name is Joan (my friends call me "Pony"). I live in a middle-sized town and belong to a middle-class family. My friends didn't dare me; the school work didn't pressure me; my parents don't drink or smoke or work late and leave me home alone . . . in fact I could have taken another path but I didn't. It was my choice.

I was thirteen when I started experimenting with dope, and at the time I attended a small private school. This diary was started early in tenth grade, when I was fourteen. When my attendance dropped and my grades hit bottom, my teachers all thought I had an emotional problem, and I believed them. It's much easier to be crazy than it is to be chemically dependent. All they saw was the quiet, withdrawn little girl that sat silent in the corner; not the angry storm of guilt and self-hatred that was tearing my heart. I think in this kind of situation most people like to stay blind.

My parents never knew how serious my dependency was until the day I was admitted to St. Vincent's Treatment Center. They never found dope on me, and I delighted in creating absurd hiding places to keep it that way. The linings of old coats, the upper mouldings over my bedroom doors . . . even the oat bin in the barn. I seemed to spend more time with the police than I did with my parents, and twice my precious hiding places were discovered, to the shock of my parents. Still they remained outwardly oblivious and I fed their enabling by telling them it was "just my head" and that dope wasn't a problem. By this time I could see that it most definitely was a problem, but I couldn't care. I saw nothing worth anything in being straight. Only madness and death in the future, and that was all I wanted. This book was written with the morbid inspiration of knowing that I would soon die, and hoping it would be published after my death. I thought people would pay more attention to what I was saying if I was dead. I needed someone to cry about me. I couldn't cry about me. I couldn't cry about myself.

On January 30 of my freshman year in high school, after months of psychological testing, psychiatrists, ministers and exorcisms, I was finally placed where I belonged – in a chemical dependency Treatment Center. I began to look at myself. Not right away, understand, I stayed crazy and very blind right up until the middle of treatment. There were threats of being placed in a mental hospital . . . and I couldn't see what I was doing that was so wrong. Really, all that the doctors and staff were trying to do was save my life. My response to their anger was to crawl even deeper into myself and hide. Someone else's reaction may have been different, but I couldn't see or feel anything that they were saying to me. The one thing that got through to me was their love. I began to throw aside everything else and center on just that. When I saw that they were digging out these stale and painful emotions because they cared about me, things changed. I felt totally unworthy of anyone's love and I can say now that it hurt like hell for anyone to tell me that they loved me. At night before lights out we had a time of "goodnight hugs" which became very special to me. The one thing that I missed the most when I was discharged was the support that they'd given me.

Treatment also demanded a rigid schedule: up in the morning at quarter to seven, dressed and beds made by seven, Yoga until eight, breakfast and then group from nine until eleven. Sometimes after morning group a few of us would go over to Detox (that's where they put you first when you go in for treatment) to give lectures on various subjects relating to C.D. (chemical dependency).

And then there was the much-whispered-about "Ugly Family" that you were sure to meet sometime during your stay. Sometime near the middle of February I met them. One by one the residents were led into the group room followed by loud crashings, clangings, and screams. My turn came. I was instructed to close my eyes, sit down, and put my head on my knees. There was much pan-clanging, spoon-drumming, and other all-out battle noises before I was told to sit up. Around me were the other residents, sitting stock still. "What is this?" I laughed nervously. The room thundered. "What is this?" they all repeated. I cringed. They cringed. I shifted. They shifted. I was being confronted with my own defenses. Eventually I was silent, and they gave up on me. Some people had many imaginative solutions. One girl spoke in Spanish, and one boy jumped on a chair and ripped his shirt off. As you can imagine, this was a biological obstacle for many of us. Literally a real show-stopper.

Occasionally there would be alternatives to group. Sometimes we'd all go down for Church in the chapel, or Brent Wiser (he's a Christian youth leader) would bring up some friends and give us a concert. One time we had to make our own commercials on chemical dependency. The "Trust Falls" were a favorite on the ward. A person would stand up on a table and fall down backwards into a crowd of people. The trust comes from believing your friends will support you. There was a lot of warmth. Hugs, backrubs, and a thing we did in group called "sense." One person would lie down on the floor while another would touch his or her face and hands. The person in the middle had to guess who it was that was touching them. They could usually tell if the person was angry or uncomfortable by what kind of touch they had. One Indian girl, for instance, could tell the touch of a very prejudiced boy who had been confronted on his behavior towards her. "Cold," she said. "I knew it was him because he was so cold."

During both Treatment and Detox there was occupational therapy which was very useful to me. I'd always been so afraid of failing that I'd seldom finish anything I'd started, but in "O.T." we had to finish one thing before we started another. I found out that I could really do something and have it turn out nicely. I made a parade bridle for Seiche, my horse, out of a plain cowhide, and a poster on feelings depicted by cartoon horse faces. Slowly, very slowly, I was growing. I remember the first time I stepped outside on my discharge day . . . it was like I'd never seen anything before. Everything was a new experience, and often a scarey one.

Treatment is only half the battle. The rest is on the outs. There were the old junkie friends, the pushers and partyers and a raw, open world ready to shovel me up and dump me back in. Probably the loneliest time in my life was right after Treatment. Daycare took up my weekdays for about a month, when I got a job as a waitress in a pizza shop. It was a neat responsibility, and I began to meet new friends and make "new connections" as we'd called them in Treatment.

It was a beautiful summer. I attended a camp that I'd been going to for years and really went all out. Dancing, art, sailing, riding, etc. I'd never thought before that I could tackle that many things and do well in each of them. Thanks to the understanding of two very neat ladies that ran the place, I was well-accepted and not penalized for my past. It meant a great deal to me.

The first day of school was a milestone. A few people I'd known in Treatment, Artful Dodger, and Dan, my old boy friend, sort of huddled together all day. We were terrified. Maybe "threatened" is a better word. One old junkie came up to me with speed and dumped it in my hand. "Here," he said. "I owe ya." With steady hands I marched into the bathroom and flushed it away. It felt . . . well, fantastic! That was probably the turning point from my faded outlook on life.

This book is real. The misspelled words are mine. The language is real. Some people may find it offensive, but I couldn't say it any other way. My responsibility is for my life, now, and the real me starts breaking through my defiance when I say I'm thankful to God for it still being here.

And this book isn't really a book. It's a diary (my diary). Four years ago I would have cursed anyone that read a single page. It was my hiding place. I can't hide there anymore. Now I'm just hoping that someone will see that there is another road to take. It may seem distant and awfully dark and lonely, but it's there. If this diary only gets through to one person, it will have been all worth it to me. That person who's lonely and desperate and needs help . . . that person who can't tell the trap of their own mind from hell itself . . . this book is for you. You have my prayers. It'll take guts and God to get you there, but you *can* get there. This is for the person who's ready to fight with his or her very self to be free. This is for the person who's ready to tear off a huge piece of self and stand back and cry a little and say . . .

I have to stand up now. I have to leave you. It's time to go home.

I never saw the sun rise . . .

Up early, and finding it deliciously devious from my usual schedule, I basked in the corral of extra time. I never saw the sun rise this morning. My heart soon caught up with the scrambling of my mind, and they raced on together, anxious for nothing. This feeling is a mother to me; I've felt it for so long. Maybe longer, not realizing it before. On through the tragic routine; the dogs shuffle in the hall, waiting to spring for goodmorning when the doorknob turns . . . the horsey-smelling coat pulls on tight over fat arms . . . the snow complains in unity with my feet, and the colt blinks and stretches to the sudden light. At once I, being a hideous escapist, reach into my pocket for the hard, cold bottle that will make painful reality go away. My sanity didn't last long.

I walked to Country Kitchen for coffee, but I wasn't hungry. My hunger could only be satisfied by talking to certain people — Kevin for one — but no one was there. Time wasted by, spent playing with straw wrappers and ash trays, drumming my fingers on the counter, watching the time too fast slip away . . .

Once here at school, I see the halls papered with children, and hear the drums beat spirit to the band for the game tonight. I seem to have missed getting involved, but I couldn't be there if I tried, my mind flies so . . .

Every weekday I take a step backward, not looking where I go . . . And my presence is supposed to mean something here? I just return to this wherever-I-am place of being after three o'clock.

The harder my head tries to catch my soul, the farther they drift apart. My infamous "rut" is my whole life. But now my fear of failure builds such tremendous ladders to success that they're surely also built on weakness. They can't last. Why this anxiety of "not doing" that I feel? I find it sad to recognize that I'd rather leave things unfinished than fail when I try. I've heard it said that "we can do nothing of ourselves" without God, and God is certainly in exile from my heart. Still, that's just a good excuse. I'd thought until now that this God syndrome of mine came in one big chunk of confusion. But no, it's laced in delicately with a "worldly" life and I can't go back and splice my life like a movie film. There are too many hills and holes in it that are nothing; they make no sense. They make me crazy.

I think of how I've spent almost all of my life; bells clanging — ordering to another room, another thought, another day or night. There's something so totally ironic — but exactly what I can't tell. Just one tragic comedy on top of another . . . and more. That shouldn't seem so funny. It's sad, really. Very sad that I'm still fighting the jagged adversary that most have given in to — reality. This body will never grow old, oh no . . . But oh, how this mind is rushing to death in its desperate fight for acceptance. Please day, slow down . . .

I never saw the sun rise . . .

I NEVER SAW THE SUN RISE

Part one

The panic of all I know

Summer, before tenth grade

Alright, now that I'm alone, I've got to think. I've got to find myself. Self: You are 5′6″, have blue eyes, brown hair, and a fair complexion (with freckles). You are fairly straight. You are just like everybody else. You are naturally quiet, but love to be happy and let everyone know it. Rowdy!! You have some good friends . . . You lie, more than you'd like to; you don't want to at all. You know some cops, and some are your friends, some are not. You have smoked weed, cigs, drunk vodka, booze, peppermint schnapps, wine, champagne, whiskey, brandy. You have been serious about killing yourself. Other times you thought you were, but you weren't.

You really loved a man. And you were really hurt. The last time you saw him he was walking down the road carrying a suitcase. He didn't answer when you called. He was twenty-five, you were fifteen. You were both crazy. But you loved him, and he didn't know how to love you. Now that you think about it, if he were here with you, you would do whatever he said, you would be scared, but you know you need him. You wish he was back, but there's something strange about the two . . . him leaving right when you begin to feel this way. You begin to wonder if you'll ever love again.

You are confused. Some people say crazy.

You love your parents, but they're both children still. You hate them enough to leave them, but you love them enough not to. You are torn. You love your brother, but have been told that he is "braindamaged" from drugs. He loves you, but is sad and agressive — now that he's straight — because he knows you're doing exactly what he did. He has to stand back and watch, and hope, like you did. You love your relatives, but don't understand or have enough time for them. You are sorry inside, but outside nothing changes. You must be selfish, then.

You are as your brother was; and what seemed so awful to watch him do isn't so awful when you're living it. You don't understand . . . You have been told you were withdrawn, when all along you thought you are very open and honest. That hurt you. But you will be as you are and you will not change for *their* thoughts. You are stubborn, then.

You wish to be thinner, and you don't really try. You are sensitive and smart about actions, gestures and body language. You read people's thoughts. You believed in God, then no one, now the devil, and God when you need him. You are a witch. The leader of your local coven. You wish to run away for the hell of it, as you consider cat and mouse games fun, and as you are good at them. But you are afraid of your parents. You are *not* afraid of the police. At times they are pigs, cops and hard-asses. Other times, they are friends, protectors, and you need them.

Same as your religion, this works the same way. They (the cops) are there when you need them, as God is when you need him. Someday you'll want them and they won't be there. And you wonder why. You need to think ahead, then.

You believe in your heart that you could be headed for, or are already in, trouble. You are the type that could be a tramp, you would throw your love about; be used. You could become seriously addicted to speed; and you could OD some night and wind up dead. You want real friends, not plastic ones. You believe (and you know) you are dangerously lonely. You believe you need some type of help, but you won't ask for it anymore.

You have been let down, and lied to, and above all, not believed when you tell the absolute truth. You have been told that you must help yourself before any other help can come to you. You believe you can't live the way you did before, you believe you have affected your brain. You know inside that you are scared, and want friends like the friends at camp. The people that won't think you just want attention when you cry, the people that understand, the people *you* understand. The people that tell each other everything's going to be alright . . .

• • •

I go home to my room, for that is all I live in at my "home" supposedly. I find that, no, I am not as straight as I was, but rowdier, and more frightened, but more daring anyway. I know well what this means. More of what I was and less of what I should be and more of what trouble is, but no death, no death.

• • •

On my way again. Going to juvenile court this time. Thanks to [Officer] Hubert. Hubert's Bag Service. You tag 'em, we bag 'em. Curfew, in the water this time. On my way, straight but rowdy. Think I'll run away.

He always got us for curfew, and that was one law I never *did* obey . . . If anything happens to me while I'm breaking the law, that's cool, because I guess I deserve it. But again, he gave us too many warnings and we heard him but maybe couldn't percieve him busting us after befriending us. Hell, that idea's changed. I know that you can't ignore laws because you happen to know the cop that's working. If you expect him to ignore you breaking the law because he's your friend, then you're really not his friend at all. A cop in Spring Valley told me that. He and I get along pretty good . . . he said if you ever give him the chance to bust you, then you're simply not his friend because he doesn't *want* to bust a friend at all. But we pay the police through our taxes and most of them do a damn decent job for it. We pay them to work for us, and protect us, but we can't really mean that if we expect them to bust "evil-doers" and not ourselves . . .

But, instead of listening to what the cop I was previously mentioning [Hubert] said about curfew, we just avoided him as much as possible after 10:00 and did what we damn well pleased even so. "On with the night, she is still young!" was our motto after 10:00. We just had an added extra of having to ditch anything that looked like cherries (roof lights) or Ford headlights, or sounded like a cheap tweety Ford engine at night. We ditched everything but Volkswagons, because only a V-dub sounds and looks like a V-dub. The rest we couldn't be sure of. "Pig," whenever any of us heard that, we were off like a shot. And so was the pig. He didn't have to get out and run; in most cases his searchlight would reach us as far as we could run . . . I know he'd seen us before when we ditched. He didn't say anything, but tried to ignore us. I think we were pretty hard to ignore. A bunch of rowdies hiding behind a tree with a 6-inch radius. Real criminal minds we were!

Anyway, on this one day Sadie cut a buouy away from the guide ropes at the Robbins beach. It was the day after I got home from camp where I had been for a month . . . Sadie left and went home and I stayed in the life guard chair on the dock. There was no one else there at the time except two guys who were walking down the beach toward me. Earlier, Sadie and I had left a note on the new squad car which was parked and locked unattended. It said something like, "Hubert, we were here but now we're gone, vandalized squad car, come to Robbins Beach if you want to get out of this alive," and signed it, "us." The letter made no sense, as we hadn't touched the squad car except to put the note under a windshield wiper, and Hubert (the cop) didn't have anything to get out of, dead or alive, but we wrote it and put it there anyway. I think I must have been feeling rowdy, it being my first day on the town and out of a forest in a month. Hubert came down to the beach in the old unmarked just as the boys that were on the beach pulled out a shiny metal tool (a knive?) and were in the process of examining ropes. "Being sneaky today in an unmarked, huh?" one asked, straightening up nervously. "Yeah," Hubert said, waved and drove on. He hadn't seen me sitting there. The sun was behind me.

So goes the lit part of the day.

At about 9:45 we decided to pull Cherries Foster down to Sadie's and go swimming at her dock (Sadie's dock) . She lives one dock away from this beach it just so happens, and it was 10:00 already by the time were were in the water.

I hadn't been worrying about curfew, being in Whitefish, Minnesota, in the forest, and I think I was "night-spoiled." That is, tramping around at night with no consequences whatsoever. There just aren't searchlights in forests. (There aren't any in Whitefish either, for that matter.) We rowdies always ran around in thunderstorms and pulled fuses from the boxes on the different cabins. Then proceeded to use kazoos to scare the pants off the campers. (A certain mouth movement ommitted a "skunk-growl.") And they never knew if it was real or not, as the rain brought out multitudes of the little black-and-white creatures from every hole in the ground. (They must have had the biggest skunk population of any town ever planted with wildlife.)

Speaking of black and white (even though the squad was blue and white) and finally getting back to the subject, we decided to have one more long distance swim to the beach and back. Super ignorant mistake (and what would have been a lot worse, we almost went skinnydipping). This searchlight fingers around the corner and immediately landed on us. Meanwhile, we were swimming our asses off toward Sadie's property. I've never moved quite that fast in the water for a long time. I was underwater most of the time and still I was lit. Sadie had disappeared, (she swims like a fucking fish) and Foster and I were chugging along like a couple of turtles. Then Sadie, like a dip, goes and yells, "It's Hubert!" Her voice is unmistakable, and he didn't mistake it. He was on foot, with a flashlight running on the shore. We hadn't figured on that at all, and he ran out on the middle dock and caught Foster right in the face with his Ray O' Vac. "Turn around, Donlan," she said. My face was away, and he didn't have the slightest idea who I was, and I considered one last burst of topflight speed derived from pure fear, but Foster could not deny the fact that I was with them, so I turned.

"Hello, Hubert. Evening," I said, finally giving in. Flash! Right in the pupils. Momentarily blinded both of us.

"Stay," he says, pointing an accusing finger at us. "Sadie," he yelled. "I'm going to call your folks if you don't come back here right now. I caught your friends." Sadie didn't realize there was no escape and her knieving mind was racing. About 9 yards behind the dip was a water patrol boat trying to figure what was pulling off at the beach. Sadie sat real still and tried to make like a buouy. Unfortunately, she was five times over her head and eventually sunk like a rock. Buouys just don't sink like rocks, and of course, the water pigs knew it. She started back.

Meanwhile on shore, Foster and I wade through knee-deep decayed seaweed and leeches, and Hubert motioned us to follow him. I absolutely read his next action like it was pre-recorded. He turned and walked dutifully off the dock. He heard Foster getting out of the water and immediately spun around and zapped her with the Ray O' Vac. Now for those of you who don't know Foster, I think I'd better attempt to describe her. She was wearing a very, very low cut bikini (the one that her mother wouldn't wear in the daylight hours) and her nickname is "Cherries." I'll leave it at that and let your imaginations figure the rest. So she turns red and gets out on the docks. (Hubert had a supressed grin from ear to ear, in fact, the only ear to ear grin I've really ever seen is that one. He has a very rounded smile even when he's not looking at a wet chick in a bikini.) And I walked out through the water, glad that Sadie has warned me of the problem with the bikini I had borrowed from her that night. It had no elastic on the bottom half and (to say the least) practically fell off as I left the water.

"Make sure to go out that way so I can't see you," said Hubert. I flipped him a casual bird in the darkness. He piled us in the back of K2, which was the old squad car, and was now unmarked. I remembered then that the last time I had been back there was when Brendan (another cop, our friend) used to talk with us. Hubert's jacket was sat upon by Foster and I slid next to her. Hubert kept the searchlight on Sadie as she emerged next to a tree. I ain't woman's lib too much, but one thing I hate is a pig who opens the *back* door of a squad car, bows slightly and waves his hand twards a temporary jail behind a dog kennel screen that seperated us. And thus, three juveniles, or should I say "wet" juvenile delinquents, were crammed into a warm squad car back kennel and awaited the pig's oink (his decision of what the hell to do with us). Then he turns on the air conditioner full, and it was a cold summer's night anyway. As far as mottos go, this one applied damn good here. "One smart-assed turn deserves another." And we got pretty smart-assed. THAT . . . now THAT!! was a real mistake!

"Who cut the ropes?" asks Hubert.

Silence. "They were like that," someone said.

"What ropes?" someone else said.

I think I stayed out that round. He shined the searchlight at the ropes, or what was left of them. They were cut into foot long segments and were floating all over the place. Oh great. That made us look good. As far as smart-asses go, it takes one to know one, I say. Hubert left and looked for incriminating evidence. And then he turns on a cassette recorder in the front seat. We just figured what he can't hear won't get him ticked, so we proceeded (through chattering molars) to degrade him as much as possible. The language itself wasn't that bad to us, just street talk. Hubert didn't apparently think so when he returned to the village hall to play it. He told us to tie the ropes, and we did, then said to go. "That way," he said, pointing toward our original escape route, and we did that too.

He should have heard us then. "Jeez, do I feel like a fucker," Cherries said, through easy side stroke movements. "Shit, yeah," said a person who pleads the fifth. "We don't deserve to get out of this."

Sadie was silent in slipping yard by yard ahead of us. "I don't understand it. Why is he letting us off? I mean, that's cool but we deserved an all-out bust."

"He's sweet," Cherries said, matter-of-factly.

I silently agreed. Until the phone rang at Sadie's and he informed them (her parents) that he was sending us to court. That's the way it goes. Now I don't quite know what to expect from any pig. Just, in any case, don't return a smart-ass comment or gesture with anything but, "officer so-and-so, please-please, thankyou, I'm sorry." And the like. It shows you where I am with law and authority . . .

July 25

Wrote Brendan a letter. Got a ride from Detective Reddy. Saw the movie *Dirty Mary/Crazy Larry.*

If I thought I was confused before, look at me now. It's straight or burnt, rowdy or quiet, trouble or peace, love or hate, friends or enemies.

HELP.

I love you, Brendan. How can I repay what you've done for me? How can I tell you I'm sorrier than I've ever been in my life? Can I ever make things right again? If not, it's my fault. If yes, it's your doing. For all you've done you deserve a medal. And then we went and blew it. Don't think I haven't been aware of what was going on. You don't know what a mess it turned out to be. We told Sadie more than once about how obviously she wanted attention. Then she was my enemy. The same thing happened with all of us. I don't know if you remember that creepy diary of mine, but it mentions all of that way back in October. It hasn't gone unoticed. But it has gone unpunished. Until now, with all of us. If I have hurt your patience, I'm so sorry.

No more jokes. I can see "it's all over," like Hubert said, and I didn't want these things to go unsaid.

Aug. 8

Came back from One Way Camp and this is the second time I've had to write this because some people at some church ripped out most of the pages because they thought there were demonic forces behind them. They burned Seiche's [Seiche is my horse] tail-hair necklace. Then they told me to sell Seiche. They think I use him to call the demons.

LET ME OUT OF HERE.

I was supposedly posessed up there, so they did an exorcism on me in a trailer. Wierd. There were two dark cats in front of it, and one gave me this strange look. Then they tried to get me to say, "I denounce the devil and all his evil ways," and I flipped out. My head went heavy, my eyes couldn't focus, and I started hyperventilating, then growling and screaming.

I held on to a piece of my head to remember with . . . Got back to the tent at 3:30 in the morning. That afternoon, we drove to the town hall and did the same thing again. "Soani" the demon, went from me to O.K. (a counselor) and back to me again. Went home pretty confused.

The Panic of All I Know

The grayness raises the roof
off the mystery
and the sun shines in . . .
the panic of all I know grips me and
I want to shake people
and tell them how
blind they are . . .
Another store window flashes an innocent sign
and they joke
and the panic of all I know
makes me crumble and I
die inside,
screaming . . .
Oh-dear-world-what-you-don't-know!
It's becoming a fad.
The darkness closes the doors
and sinks down upon us
and the Devil
smiles in . . .
Then the panic of all I know makes me tell them.
It is finished.
They laugh and walk away.

Tuesday night

Returned Pig Roy Wilhelm's phone call and he said I wouldn't be allowed on the ride-along for six months. O.K. called. Saturday she and her dad and Ed Deforest and some pastor did the same deliverence bit again and that's when they wrecked my diary.

Now it's Tuesday, the 12th. Det. Reddy just toured me to Harding High School. It'd cost us 1500 bucks. Too much for too little. I'll probably end up at Willowood High School. What a bitch.

First I heard that the police were for protecting people from each other. Then I heard that the police were for protecting people from themselves. Now I'm wondering who's there to protect *me* from *myself?*

All I want to do right now is get loose — I'd like to toke a million bowls. No, I just want to be with Simon. But I think I've forgotten his home number — it's too much like the Spring Valley city hall's. That's all I need to do — get those numbers mixed up.

R-R-R-R-R-ing.

"Hello."

"Hey, boy, let's boogie."

"Who is this?"

"Pony. Who else?"

"Well, this is Chief."

GASP.

CLICK.

You know what I mean.

(Letter I forgot to send)

Detective Reddy,

Following your request, I have only this to say.

The kids in my class, the kids I knew, the kids I don't know, no matter how much they hate me, they are still my friends. And there's no possible way that I'm going to narc on them just because you don't have enough busts on your record. Or for any reason. So yeah, I might join the police academy when I'm 18. But that is then, and this is now. I'm not 18 yet, and I'm not straight yet, and my friends aren't really my friends, but they are also no better than I am. I do the same things they do. So one question. Why do you think I'm different from them? Because I talk to you? I talk to you because I think you're a good guy. No more, no less. I won't be a narc.

Pony

Thursday, 15th

Thought pour le day.
BREAD AND JELLY,
PEANUT BUTTER
AND GUNPUPPY

horses / cops /
feeling /
friends /
weather /
names / places

I've been;
realistic or
imagined /
situation /
bad or good

August 23

I sat at the bowling alley and then I walked and it was late but not late enough to be worried — there was that same feeling in the air — the lights — the wind — the dark — the stars — the peace. Just like how I like to go and sit in phone booths. You can watch people and they don't care about you. They leave you alone. Brendan passed us and didn't honk or wave or anything. We followed him to the bowling alley and he was not there . . .

I sat and looked at squad car K2 and tried to remember the way it was and the way we were a long, long time ago. We time things by events and not by time alone. In that sense, I feel I should be in my grave. Called the Hotline and they were busy. Called Fries [a friend] and she wasn't home . . . it got very lonely.

AND I DON'T WANT ANY HELP.

August 26

I'm staring at the incredible length from my eyes to my feet. I'm thinking of how long [a time] it really must have been, though it seems so short. I'm talking of growing old. I see what's happened. I understand. I won't let it be too late.

Wednesday, August 28

Met the cop named Roy Wilhelm at Country Kitchen yesterday (with Trella). Saw him today at Bridgeman's (tonight). He's cool. (For a cop.) Ponied colt behind Seiche on frontage (road). I'm lonely and I'm sad and I wish to hell I could just cruise all night and there was no curfew or people that hurt you. I wish they'd just stick me in a mental hospital. Hell, I feel like I deserve it. I need it. I'd like to be locked into my little square room with a chair, a board for a desk, and a bed. I'd like to just sit there and think and be counted as a number, not a person. Maybe sometimes they'd forget me and leave me alone. And if I got a room with a window for good behavior, I'd stare out at night and look at the stars . . .

I don't think this is really happening

AUGUST 30!!

Orientation at Willowood High. Football game at Clairdale.

C-L-A-I-R-D-A-L-E

! ! ! ! ! !

Short as hell game. Pigs on EVERY corner of EVERY block in EVERY forest by EVERY dark area and EVERY fence . . .

Saturday, and I have no idea what day it is. I just broke a toe and I'm at our cabin up north and I've been driving the Pontiac and I hate Willowood High School and I hate Winthrop [the private school] — and I can't get away from the old routine of school, dope, memories, Satan . . . and whenever I think of another year I also think of being committed to a sanitarium or a grave. God or Satan or dope or facing reality or living or dying or truckin' or stayin' or bad or good or trying to figure out what the hell I'm talking about . . .

I told Mom. She deserves to know what's killing me. She deserves to know where I'm going when I die. She deserves the truth. And Satan makes me hate it. I'm in for it tonight.

Sept. 4

Roy read a lot of this garbage. He didn't read any of the bad stuff. Damn it!!!! He's cool and everything but I'm doing what I did with Brendan. Trying to figure myself out. I can't. See, that in itself flips me out . . . He asks me what the hell's my hang-up. IF I KNEW MY HANG-UP I WOULDN'T BE SO BUMMED OUT. Oh, screw it, why don't I just forget it — I've tried too damn long and I just can't hack it. I'll see if I can work in an extra suicide along with the murders this month. So mote it be.

Sept. 5

I guess they'll all just sit here hoping that I'll change. I look at myself as a terminal case. Went out with Lou and Stash Hannon. I went out with Rico Michelson who ain't bad. Saw Denny LaVerse. I heard the dogs barking, and I didn't figure much of it. I walked back into the barn and he was just standing there. What a rush. Wants me to come out sometime. "To talk cars?" I asked. "Yeah, or whatever," he answered. Dick Cavett looks like Simon. Rico M. is cool . . . Didn't see Roy today. Trella called. Cherries called. "She sells" (written by teacher on the blackboard) got my fear started in French class. I'm getting some speed Friday. My biology teacher is a pig.

Still Thursday, Sept. 5

Double cruised — Lou and Stash and Rico and I. Went to municipal liquor store and got turned down. Roy cruised by. Drove around. Went to The Music Store and got a "Rush" sticker.

Friday, Sept. 6

I think I'm in love. Rico's the kind of guy that *will* take no for an answer. I think I've found someone that's not just out for the sex. I think I can trust him. We went to the CLAIRDALE FOOTBALL GAME. Pigs all over. Went to hill and imitated pig stance. Saluted when he did. Did a "hail" Hitler sign. Walked around him in a circle chanting, "Blessed Be."

Saturday, Sept. 7

Rode Seiche. Ate at A&W with Rico. Went home and he got drunk and wouldn't stop drinking. He started making out and I think I'm going to have to say Goodbye. He's too much trouble . . .

Called Kevin [he's a Jesus-lover cop] at 2:28 a.m.

Sunday, Sept. 8

Woke up at 11:30. Rico called. Went back to bed. Called Rico. Went to party. Didn't drink. Rico did; he got drunk.

Went out in the boat. Siren and Cherries swamped the canoe. Their boyfriends Dan and Preston saved them. Rico and I played disc-jockey-on-the-roof. Someone threw Trella in. Someone threw me in. Sadie threw Rico in. Rico threw Sadie in. Everyone got everyone in. Came home. Went to grandparents' with Sunny [my brother's Shetland sheepdog].

Now Kevin wants me to convert. I won't. I'm afraid of people, so I use my Satanism. People are afraid of things they don't understand. The devil protects me from people through their fear of his power. Jesus can't protect me from people because people aren't afraid of love. Only *I* am afraid of love. "The devil believes in revenge," I tell them. And they stay away from me. All of them . . . So I am alone. And sometimes that's fine. But most times it's lonely. And I can't think of what I should be doing. I'm confused, paranoid, doubting.

Alright, Jesus, I've heard it from both sides, a little you, a little them. I'm confused in a different way with the different people involved. I want to hear more from you. Please Jesus, if I asked you to come into me would you stay there and help me with these jokes I've created? Would you help me to make the most of what I am? See I have these doubts; some people say it's Satan that's giving me these doubts. Others say there is no Satan. Others say that it's a cop-out blaming your emotions or actions on Satan. Don't you see that I don't know who I am? I don't feel as if I'm a person at all. I want to be at peace with myself.

Like now, I think Satan's saying — you don't want to write in this — "Fuck it" I heard him say. Or was it him? Was it me? Who am I? Where would I be if I'd stayed where I was when I was straight? Where would I be if [my brother] Tom hadn't found Jesus? Where would Tom be without Him? What's going to happen to me and Rico? Can you help me change Rico? I just want to find myself. So right now I'm asking you to come into my heart and do with my life as you see fit. No. Hell with it.

SMILE SMILE SMILE
SMILE SMILE SMILE
SMILE KEEP ON SMILIN'
Schooled Seiche. He jumped pretty well, high at least.

Friday the 13th

Bullshit, man, that's all. Lou called — said Rico thought I hated him. I thought he hated me so Stash got ticked at her and went to the football game with me and met Rico who was supposed to be meeting me and *he* got mad and Tom came with his friends to be a Pig Brother and we said we were going to leave and we did so he followed us to make sure we were going where we said we were going . . . and not to that "cannibel meeting" he'd "heard about."

Exorcism. At One Way headquarters. Kevin came all the way from Granchester for nothing.

10 to 2 in the morning and Mother says, "You have nice friends," and I felt like slapping her face . . .

Saturday the 14th

Took off. Came back to barn loft. Circle [of chairs] broken. Couldn't feed horses. Too scared to go out there . . .

Thursday

Stayed home — Walked Seiche / vet / colic / colt cast in stall.

Friday, Sept. 20

Homecoming parade. We lost. I want to know where I am because I don't think this is really happening. I think I'm crazy and I belong in a hospital because I want to die and I want to kill and I want to love and that must mean that my mind's pretty gone.

Monday, Sept. 23

Joan, she says when I open this [diary], Joan, dinner's ready. So I close the book and blow out the candles, and again all is as it was. All is dark.

Skipped school again and I'll probably flunk everything in it. Stash and Lou and I went to Country Kitchen and then to the mall, then to the library. We saw that Kevin was there. Lou went out and talked to him. Stash said that Mom said that all of this was happening because I was "mentally disturbed" after Tom's experiences. Lou said the same thing. She really doesn't believe it. She really thinks I am crazy. I'm so tired of trying. It's the demons. The same thing happened when Christ died for us. People weren't ready to accept him as He was, His ideas; even though it was truth.

The same thing's happening here. Mom can't believe it because they (the demons) won't let her. I thought most of us were ready. I was very, very wrong. You can see it's a struggle. It takes more faith and more will than I can muster. It doesn't show outside, not at first, but the mind can't house so much power and grief. Eventually you notice that some of it is seeping out and if no one is there that knows what's wrong, ZAP, it can kill you. Really kill you. The people today don't condemn you to death for that, they condemn you to a padded cell. I begin to wonder which one is worse, you know? It really tears you apart. You have to face disbelievers, Satan, yourself, friends . . . for the first time I've had to sort out my friends and judge them. I won't mention names here. Now Mom is making me go to all these Christain things and if she keeps pushing it I'm going to have to take off because when I think about it, maybe I *am* crazy and I know they treat me like I am.

I have no idea whether this is me or one of *them,* but I do know that whoever I am or it is doesn't want me to do another exorcism. It's fine when I'm by myself. But mainly it's just Mom. She's so damn joyful that her darling daughter has come "home" that she won't leave me alone and consequently, *they* won't leave me alone. She goes out and buys me this cross and then sets up all these appointments with some pastor and has to know where I'm going every minute of the day even if I'm going to the barn and it gets so bad that I just leave at night sometimes. You can't force any religion on a person. It doesn't work that way, if it works at all. It should be my decision, not hers. The more she pushes it, the weaker I get. I want to let it be me that helps myself. I want to have the will. I want nothing done for me by anyone but Jesus.

They'll have to learn it's just not something you can force.

It takes time.

So what do I do about this? Sadie calls and asks for Kevin's phone number. Which I'd almost consider giving her because he would try to fill her with the Spirit. But I know her. And while he was doing that, she'd be filling him with bull. I want her to be happy, but not if it hurt someone that's a better friend to me anyway.

• • •

Mom: "Oh God!"
Me: "What?"
Mom: "Why did you put those black light posters up again? They're so fierce."
Me: "They are not fierce."

Tuesday

I felt in my jacket pockets for a pen and I found that they were empty. So I turned and feasted my eyes on the baggie by my bed. An original official-type drug-and-whatever confiscating pig bag. I open it and find a pen and think, "What a day."

Left school before lst [period], went to Willowood Country Kitchen and had coffee with Stash. Then, as we watched pig chief drive by, I left, he left; We went our seperate ways. I sat in the field and watched the Bird [our barn pigeon] cruise around above me. And I wished I could be that free. Went home. Mom left. Called Det. Reddy and rapped with him. He was his usual "self." Called Brendan and got someone who started to give me his number, then he said he'd tell him to call me. I waited. I prayed to Jesus that He'd give me the words to say that might fill Brendan with the Spirit. And I waited, but he didn't call.

Mom told me to call Brent Wiser [this Christain youth leader], so I did, and by the time he called me back, McKenzy septic people were there [in our front field] and so was Rico. I didn't get much said. Then (or was it earlier?) Lou called and said she was going to the bank and did I want to go? I said no, anyway. So she and Stash left. Come back around 5:30. Lou was drunk. Stash reeked of weed. I put on my Rag [my old army coat] over my ski jacket and didn't bother to clean out the pockets. I loaded the Pentax Camera and hung it around my neck. We trucked to the bowling alley via the thumb. Got a ride with some dude that had a van with loose sides and wobbley seats and John Denver tapes.

Took some pictures. I was just taking pictures of the bowling alley sign, and Lou yells, "If you want to get high, come on." And I didn't want to toke, but I went with them and Neil. Took some pictures and left (after toking). Took a picture of a bowling alley sunset. Neil asks me if I know anyone that wants 3 bucks of dope, shows it to me, and I turn around. Nosing off from the tar stalls comes this blue as hell Ford front and then a license plate that was tax exempt and orange and by this time I was thinking, "Oh no." And "Pig," I said and I catches sight of some cherries. "We're busted," said Neil. And we were.

Pig thought I'd stolen the camera. He busted Neil first, and he sat him down. And we were searched and he treated us like dogs and put his pig jacket on me. "Squad 62" sticks us in his car and peels for the hall. They locked us in a little cement room with a peephole and a two-way mirror and took our jackets and we froze.

We finally figured that it was Stash and Neil through that damn window. So we set up this code of knock-knock. Drove the pigs crazy.

Lou had to go to the can. She knocked on the door. Big-as-all-hell detective takes her out. She comes back.

"You gotta go too?"

"Yeah," I says. So I go down to the end of the hall. Through here, he says, and he followed me, and I'm thinking, "how far is he coming in?" And I was in a pig dressing room and he says, "Right around the corner," and I go in there and there are copies of pig magazines in there. I mean, like police journals and Minnesota Consolidated Pig, etc., on the back of the can. I try to ignore the fact that there's a pig standing right in front of me. Went back to my cozy little room with the warm, warm cement walls, floors and everything else but the ceiling which seems to be there to kick in.

Fucker No. 1 says, "Lou, would you come with me, please?"

So I sit there and I try to pray, and all that comes out is, "Jesus, where were you today?"

Lou comes back crying. "I'm going to jail," she says. "I'm going to jail. I need 100 bucks for bail quick."

So we sit and freeze and finally I get to go home. I can't picture Lou behind bars tonight. She doesn't deserve it.

So here I am, staring at the pig bag. I'm about to see what I got left.

1 pig wallet (mine), slightly smashed
1 show program w/Brendan's parents' phone number
9 match books (make that 10)
1 brush
1 pack of cigs
1 film cannister
1 unopened film
1 hoof pick
a pocket knife
1 bottle of Visine
1 ripped-off camp swimming buddy tag
1 pill box
2 dollar bills
67 cents in loose (very loose) change and I'm about to see if those fuckers took my film from the camera.

123 AHH, 321, WHEW!

It's still there. I'm about to cut myself and let it bleed and if I die that's my problem. Goodnight, Pony, you loser. You're such a loser.

(Mrs. Donlan, be glad I had but a blunt scalpel.)

peering through the cage
of a police squad (when
knowledge of his coming might have freed us)
all we saw was the cage that
held us and the locked door all we heard
was the static of the radio and
our own hearts beating all we felt
was hatred and revenge
(when knowledge of his coming might have
freed us)

Wednesday, Oct. 2

Never been laid so low, because all I DO is hurt people. I lie to them. I scare them. I don't think I can say I even deserve to live because I can't think straight and it's getting to the extreme of getting killed. Cris hates me. I hate myself. It looks like I used him. I was just crazy all along. But I'm trying as hard as I can to pray for Kevin Adams and his wife, Lisa, and the baby.

I just hope I'm not a curse.

Thursday, Oct. 3

Court. Lou's on one year's probation. Gave five riding lessons [to little kids] — (ride 'em cowboy) . . .

Friday, the 4th

. . . I was fine, then I walked down the road and I was so desperate and so scared . . . I cried and shed no tears.

Kevin's expecting Lisa to have the child tonight. I'm scared about it. I'll pray, but I'm scared. For her, for him, for the child.

Sunday, the 6th of Oct.

Baby Joy Adams almost died because of me. I don't know why. I feel a curse in my eyes . . .

Freaks that are busted together are dusted together.

I don't know.

I know nuthing, nuuthing!

Dream:

Last night I had a dream. Christ was on the cross on Calvary and everything was as it should be. Then a man in modern clothes appeared and tried to buy Him off the cross.

I was suddenly in a hospital maternity ward where Lisa's child had just been born. The nurse was upset and turned to the doctor quietly, "It is neither a boy or a girl," she said. At that moment the man in modern clothes walked in and handed me a five . . .

This whole scene is out of date

Wednesday, 10

This book doesn't mean as much as it used to. People have seen it and their eyes have made it unsacred. Without it I have no where to throw my old thoughts. So I hold them because I won't throw them at anyone because there are too many to catch. So my head blows up and gets so heavy that nothing can come out. It's like horse colic. There's nothing to do but die. Out to dinner with Brent Wiser. He's a philosopher. He is what Kevin called a Galatian . . .

Sunday, the 13th of October

What was I doing last year right now? This whole scene is out of date. Give me a hit of my memory and let me be on my way. My whole life, my memories. Just truckin' by, so I go back. Truck truck truck. It's the weather, I think. Let me relive my memories. Last year. Standing in the bowling alley door watching the snow fall down lightly. And then when Brendan came, I was always so glad. He was a welcome sight. I felt good. Now he's a grain of that old hit. I, to him, am not there at all. Or when I am, he pretends I'm not. I will not live until I find out what and why. I don't think about the future because I could give a shit about the future. I'm living back [in the past]. I ain't going ahead. I'm going to get so damn burnt out that I'm just a neutral person. I'll get some more speed from "the Spaceman."

Also Sunday

What am I going to do now? Problem. School has gotten me so psyced out that I wake up Sat. mornings and am in a cold sweat and shakey thinking I have to go there another morning. Because I'm living back, that's all I think about and I don't have time for any of this other garbage. I don't care about the future. Problem: Parents don't believe that I'm anything but lazy, but they blame it on themselves and I'm not blaming anybody so I feel guilty as hell. Problem: Religion. No one could ever believe my experiences and I don't blame them. Subproblem: Parents don't believe it, either. They think I'm crazy.

Problem: I have lost the best friend that I have ever had or will ever have and it's got to be my fault. And if I had only one night to spend here I would spend it talking to him. That's Brendan who doesn't smile anymore, or laugh. That's Brendan, who looks so sad and makes me feel so guilty. And it goes on and on.

I wrote in my notebook before I'd written a diary: You better start running. And I did. I ran from everything and hid and I'm trying to climb out of the ocean a little. It's impossible to climb in water. So instead of swimming, I keep looking for more footholds. There haven't been many since Brendan. So I keep sinking.

Problem — parts previously stated in addition to others.
Hypothesis — living back.
Date — past emotions.
Conclusion:
1. Take 2 aspirins and call Brendan in the morning.
2. Take 50 aspirins and die.
3. Die.
4. Die.
5. DIE.

Oct. 17

What a beautiful night. You shoulda been there, man. Cleaned the barn spotless. Trella over. Ray and Stash over. Super bummed. Lesson got rained out. Drew Roy's tree he asked for. It poured. Hitched back home past pig and got picked up by orange car with strange guy. "Eh???" Saw Kevin who was mad. He preached and bitched at the same time. Home. Hung up posters. Toked the BEST POT!! Trucked. Rapped with Roy . . . Put a beer can on his cherry [squad car roof light]. He drove us home. Bye freaks.

THANKS FOR THE WORRY FREE

STONE FREE NIGHT.

It's 1:30 and I should crash.

Monday, 21st of Oct.

There's no room for doubt anymore. My prayers were answered . . . Brendan is back again. PRAISE THE LORD!!

Thursday

Spatts [Sadie's horse] is hurting, I think. Can't see a fracture. But, "Do you want to put him to sleep now or later?" he said (the vet). She's going to keep trying to save him. I wish I could tell her to pray. I think it would be a good time to bring Jesus into her life. I'm praying for Spatts, but I have this feeling that God would really listen if Sadie herself would pray. Well, praise the Lord anyway, even though Spatts hurt his leg, even though I got two cavities, even though Sadie gave Brendan another note to give to "Chief" [Spring Valley police chief] . . .

Tuesday

Help. Thought me dead this morn, I did.

Thought for Simon

Standing there,
with no games left to share,
so open and fearful and proud —
not as loud,
but looking slightly like a late night show and
as hard to shut off as
a siamese cat in a door,
with no voice, and no choice,
and a bed by the floor. In the rain —
in the Tuesday night drizzle, the pain
that is etched on your face finds no peace,
nothing that I could
quite reach . . .

Thursday

Back in my room again. Red lights, incense, empty mind, people . . . moving like a river flows. People let your light shine, come on let it shine . . . it is like I can only write what I hear.

Oct. 31

Dead Hallowe'en. Died, as they should have.
POURED.

Friday, Nov. 1

Tom's CONCERT at Robinwood High School.

November 4

It's a MONDAY. Another weekend just passed. Friday night was Tom's concert. Saturday I watched *The Revenge of the Creature* and *The Strange Ghouls* and I played *Stairway to Heaven* on the piano. Sunday was horses and sick grandparents. And I'm still alive, it seems, I have promised Brent the enjoyment of his taking me out to dinner tomorrow. Wednesday is Bible study. Luke told us to come, but I wonder . . . That dream last night about the china ship, Lenny, Chris, Karen, Steve, Captain Doherty and I (just characters in my dream). Sailing around in a boat called "Time" that was made out of bone white china and the turbulent black and turquoise waters that broke the hull and drowned the chickens right in their crates in the cargo room below us.

My pen just broke. Figures, it's a Monday — Yeah, and cold as all hell again. I was in health class there, now I'm in my "quiet hour." I went riding, and showed the new neighbors around the joint. "Dick" Lucas Rogers is coming to health class Wed., a week from now. To give us a talk on drugs (gasp!) Oh gasp, gasp, gasp, drugs! (Shudder) What if the very air he moves in makes us addicts? (quake) Anyway, I thought we could simulate a bust. (That would be cute, they want to use me for a burn-out, Teri for the person I'm selling to, and Terry for the little uptight housewife.) Bye now, must truck to Target to get some clothes.

Tuesday, November 5

Bonjour! She is a Tuesday!! Non?!

It's twenty to nine and that means history soon. Another

class with brain things. I wish I could learn, but it's like there's something there, I mean . . . in front of my ears and my eyes and even my mind. Yes, especially my mind. A mind you can't fool with. It's been opened and closed and the door is stuck. That is alright, because I doubt that I want people near it anyway. I will not let anyone try to touch it with anything anymore. Brent Wiser hit a deer on the road. No, no one. I will not ask even as much as what happened to the times when I was happy? That question will not be answered by anything but the fact that today I am happier than I will be tomorrow, and that last year at this time is gone and dead in everyone's mind but mine. I can feel the air when it is like it was then. Bell ________ just rang.

Back again, yes, I can feel it. It tightens up something inside — it's that feeling, even just thinking about it, and what bothers me is that I don't understand it. Fear, maybe. When the bitter wind blows clear and sharp and my hands and face move ahead of my body in little cubes of air. When my feet in their constant frostbitten trudging through or over the snow are, too, in squares of atmosphere. Worn and scoffed, but friendly, my boots have taken my miles into myself as I walked. And the snow — powdered and crystaled like chips of styrofoam or frozen cotton, packed and rough, or black and ugly by the roadside. I have been there, I have walked there. And everywhere I went took me somewhere. Though somewhere sometimes was nowhere, it was something to see. Not a vast empty white or black, but just what I had experienced so many times before that it now meant nothing . . .

When the darkness fell, it fell gently, and bitterly cold. But my nowheres are still there, receding into black. It was quiet in my head at night. I needed only to exist, not calculate. Even the evil was not as evident as it is now.

Tuesday, November 5

I would not think of the people being killed, or cars' headlights sweeping over my boots and running up my body to my face, which stared in emptiness into them. I would wall off the voices I heard in the woods ahead of me, and the person walking far behind might seem closer but I would not let him near. I was not afraid. It came down to surviving.

Simple surviving. My head was a constant battleground and I was always fighting. Sometimes just to keep sane. Every time when I turned and saw the street light sliding over the blue and white metal and up over the red lights, there came a feeling that I can't explain because I haven't experienced it for so long. Whatever it was, I know only what it is now. Fear and sadness. At least that's what I *should* be feeling, and I *do* feel something. There are people that are still alive, actually, but in a sense, they are gone to me. Some are dead, though in my mind they live on every day. I know that it has been so long since Joella died, and was suddenly gone, and people knew what had happened — she was dead. But in people's minds she lived on, because they didn't want to believe it. And neither did I, and neither do I now. "Nothing has changed," I have said too much. But nothing has and so I say it again. But then I think and I realize that so much has changed that I don't notice it. Like the earth revolving so fast you can't tell it's moving. Like that, it happened. Maybe everything's changed. Does it really matter whether anything changes or not anymore so long as I exist? Now. Now when the darkness comes, it comes more than just at night. It comes hard, and mercilessly. It leaves no time for bringing things in to yourself to protect them. You, yourself are no longer a form of protection. You are just as endangered as a kitten in a wind storm. You are not free from death; you are an object of death. Because life is a terminal disease, anyway. Living is dying. It comes again, and it scares me. The road which is barren of snow is nowhere now. The curb in the parking lot which the first delicate line of snow drifted against is nowhere now.

The rowdy, wild, windy nights are dead, but they will never be nowhere if they are still possible if I wanted them. My wandering has stabalized. Three hundred and sixty five days ago. That's all, and it seems like three years, maybe four. I will ride on my past and it will never slip from under me for by some unexplained reason this way of life, these memories and dreams, will not perish. They remain clear in my mind and will not die. They have lived past their normal time period. They are mine forever. There's gonna be no band, no school, no people that can take my life from here. It's only me. Help. I may cry out for it, silently. I really want to die right now. Here's a juicy what-if. What if I killed myself and didn't tell anyone about it? And can't you see Brendan when he finds out? He would be in uniform, and he would just sit there and stare for a second, then maybe ask a couple of questions, and then leave it to think on later. That's it, probably.

School means either nothing or a lot. It hurts.

I want to live, not exist. Forget it, just stop it all.

I want to die.

Thursday, Nov. 7

I went to Bible Study last night and brought Sadie. Stash brought himself. Cherries brought a friend. There were between 70 and 100 people there. I left Burger King after sitting in the can because I felt sick, and I saw this black continental parked and I walked around a block and the car suddenly comes out of this little driveway and honks and spins out in the gravel. Right towards me. I just stood there and froze. I went back. Cris knows something I don't. He looked at me strangely. Luke is the only one I can trust. Stash is a narc. He was going to talk to my mom (he has before) and I will not have any more people like that because it royally screws up my life. He says he cares about me but I don't want him to because I've never really felt it before. I would rather have the kind of friend that would leave you lying in a gutter and not care shitless about it (if you call that a friend). But they don't get you in trouble because they don't get involved, and when you do get in trouble, it's just you and no one else.

I called Kevin and I told him what was going on and he says, "Just go to sleep now, Pony. Just go to sleep and don't worry."

I said, "What if I get high?"

And he said, "You do what you want to do. Go ahead and do what you want to do." And he hung up. He said he'd pray for me. Why couldn't he just talk to me? I needed someone to answer my God-questions, but I was so afraid to ask him . . . I needed to know why his God is only a cold, white stone to me . . . I needed to know why I had to be so lonely . . .

I just trucked around school and found some acid, speed

and pot. Wow! What a rush. I just got a flash from the acid and all the voices in the room slowed down to nothing, like a dead record.

LAST NIGHT TREE

Left for lunch and went home and ate a pizza, searched closets for junk, tried to open the medicine chest. Took some pills. Lit up a cig and made it to the highway and waited to cross. Roy cruises by and under bridge and I crossed. He did a U-ey and came back and I was praying for another ride (to come along) before he got there but I lost out. He honked and asked me where I was going and gave me a ride to school. I really don't like the idea of getting a ride back to school in a pig car, but no one was out front to see, so it didn't matter.

Nov. 12

I have a little zip left. Look, there's PTA people in the library and they're looking around. I should tell them there's someone stoned over here.

> If you're seeing way too much of time,
> and it won't go: You don't know . . .
> Pack away your watch and chain.
> Follow me, go where I go.

PORTRAIT

OF A

SPEED QUEEN . . . JOAN (PONY) DONLAN (the late?)

When the rabbit with the watch and the
king and the cross come together in your mind,
let them fight it out and find, who you really are
and who really made you what you are was it the
white cross or the king, you have to watch him too,
or was it the king on the cross that died but was
never high . . . or was it the rabbit king and the cross watch . . .
come together, fight it out.

Meeting the Queen

Nov. 13 - 11:05

I'm in the library because the library is such a neat place to get stoned. I can sit for hours in here and not get paranoid. Just reading the book titles and guessing the contents. I can be a burnt intellect. Maybe I'm wrong again, but I love it anyway. I love the pain this stuff gives me. Physical pain I can stand. Too bad I don't have more of it. It's the mental pain that really gouges deep. Lonliness for one [thing]. Misunderstanding for another.

I bet half of the kids at least in this school can complain of the same things I'm complaining of. All the topics. Emotions, parents, drugs, God, sex, hassles, legal stuff, bitterness, love, hate, ignorance, war, peace, truckin', stayin', flyin', crashin'. All of them. What you do is you take each of these topics, and you write why they hassle you, and what the hassle is, then you figure hard something positive about each one. That may take a while. Then you make a hypothesis and a conclusion as to what you want to do about them, and what you need to do about them. Those last two are different most of the time. So let's see . . . EMOTIONS . . . mine are locked inside all the time unless I write them, pray about them, or try to talk to a best friend about them. Why are they locked inside? . . . because I'm frightened of letting them out because there are so many of them that have been there for so long that people may think me crazy. People that know me know me to be constantly mellow. Either really mellow or really down. That's cool. I'm afraid to let them know I can really be wild in my head sometimes. There are so many ideas and strange thoughts in there that would be neat to compare with other people's. I really love people because I can read them and sympathize with them. I can relate to most of their problems. I can't really get mad outloud at people because it's so hard for me to consciously hurt someone.

11:20

Tom [when he was into dope] used to blow up a lot and he never made much sense to me then. Now he does, because I've been there too. I'd really like to talk to him about what he went through. I think maybe if I really listened to him, maybe he would finally let me talk. I feel very close to him suddenly. His music makes me want to cry and sing and laugh all at once. It's so beautiful. He's really beautiful. He's a very O.K. person and I can't help feeling that the Lord has really blessed him. His thing that has been with him all along is his music. Look at him now. Mellow, meaningful person with a head still there. I love him and I can say that easily.

My thing has always been horses, so maybe that's where I'll be. Horses are mellow, but expensive. I dig well-taken-care-of grade horses. Just plain horse, nothing fancy. I believe that you can get a grade horse to jump as well as any thoroughbred if you work him. People always asked me why I liked horses. I never really knew. Maybe for control, power; to communicate with, teach and train. Ability to talk through signals to another living thing that normally doesn't understand our methods of human communication. They [horses] understand touch, love, hate, discipline, bad and good. Through our emotions they begin to understand words. What a beautiful feeling. (A lot of animals are like that. I'm having a bit of a problem communicating with [our] tortoises. They are typically very stoney.) Or a simpler answer is that that's what the Lord made my mind close to — animals and especially horses.

But getting back again, it tore my PARENTS apart, those screwed up, rebellious years of Tom's. All the fighting. It bothered me then but I didn't often cry. I was blank. If he would have been hit by a car or killed somehow it wouldn't have effected me. That was then. Now I would look at him as an innocent victim, like so many of us. Or what if he had never come back when he took off? What if I didn't know where he was or even if he was alive? I'd probably pray for him. I wonder if he ever prays about me now. I think he knows where my head's at. See, I do love my parents. I used to communicate better, that's all. Now the typical things are in the way. Pride, rebellion, the desire to grow up and be on my own.

Love. Think once. It's still there, but all this hides it. I know the Lord had planned me to be born of these parents. So he must know everything will someday be alright. Like in the song "Get Together;" no, I guess it's "Teach Your Children." "Teach your parents well, their children's hell — will slowly go by — and help them with your youth. They seek the truth — before they can die." I want to have a good relationship with them. I want to show them I can be successful. I know I'm not dumb, but I wouldn't go calling myself smart, either. Maybe it's just that I feel I have a special understanding for people and for feelings. My writing to me is also a special gift. Because I'm so silent, [I like] to be able to write and convey meaningful thoughts on paper to others or just to myself.

He plays mellow songs, sometimes too mellow (the bus driver, I mean). He drove on Tuesdays for us at our other school last year. Same bus 14. With fiberglass seats. Lou says he is a Christain. I never knew him or talked to him much. Sometime I might like to now that I know we have something in common. Most of the Christains I know that seem to be very real Christains are meek and mellow. They may not be beautiful by the world's standards, though some are, but most seem to be either fat or out of proportion or lonely or talk funny or are silent and misunderstood. I remember, though, "Blessed are the meek, for they shall inherit the earth." I sometimes wonder if by the time we inherit it, there will be anything left of it. Anything salvageable.

I think maybe an experience with evil teaches people good. Satan is very, very sly and has unbelievable powers. But GOD is much stronger. The Bible says He is, and everything else in there is true, so why would He lie about one thing? Even now people turn to Satan in rebellion. But Satan has nothing good . . . nothing to offer better than life. He knows no love, but puts it over to his believers as love when it is actually lust. SEX fits in there perfectly. When you're married, beautiful, but you must be careful so not to let it become more important than God. There should be other ways to express love than with sex and all of them should mean as much.

You go into one of the bathrooms in this school. All over the walls you find, "LOVE." "Cindy loves Paul." "I love Dave." But it's all plastic. I can make a bet none of them have really known love. And most of their relationships are ended with sex. I once saw a piece of graffiti in a bathroom in a restaurant. "I love Jesus," it said. "Amen," I wrote. And from that point on, that certain Christain, whoever she is, and I have been leaving messages for each other in that bathroom. It is an odd way to communicate, but we always wrote in pencil, so as not to be so destructive as it does wash off. But God must have been with us because even when other things were washed off, our messages remained. The bathroom was eventually painted over, but someone, and I'll never know who . . . rewrote all of it on top of the fresh paint and it's still there.

A lot of people read the things on bathroom walls. Most of it has been said already; unoriginal, or meaningless to other people. But what we wrote applied to everyone and soon we found other Christains scrawling there, and even a few questions from non-Christains. One thing I particularly remembered was, "If you want to get high or get a good lay, call Robby at -------" some telephone number. We obviously didn't write that, but next to it we wrote, "If you want to get the best high and experience real love, call Jesus. He listens and all you have to do is pray."

I have wondered if Christains today could ever save Satan and his demons from the pit by Christain love and convert them again. An almost impossible task. God's love is so that He would forgive even Satan for his sins if Satan himself came to God and asked in truth. God also knows when you're lying. Now, even in writing this I have sinned for I am fairly high right now, but He will forgive me when I ask Him to. In fact, I have asked Him and that is where this whole subject began . . . That shows me where I really am with religion. Sometimes confused, but always sure of the One that gave me His son to die for me.

As with parents, I started to say that I know I love them, but it gets hard sometimes. Especially when they don't understand. I know that if I blew up at them it would tear them apart.

There were incidents [at home] which left me blank, and I'm glad of it because if I'd really thought about standing up for myself, I would have fought back. When I took my first multi-phasic test in mental health, it was easy and I did it fast. We were discussing a past history test on the porch during dinner one night, and all of a sudden, quite untimely, Dad pipes up, "Boy, you know one test you really blew was that first multi-phasic. You buzzed through that so fast you must not have even read the questions." I was horror-stricken. What had the result of the test been? It was as if he was looking for some consolation that I had, in fact, screwed it up intentionally. I could really read him. Very unsure, covering it up by smiling and refusing, or maybe not able to, look me square in the face.

All I said was, "Yeah." They won't let me be insane. Even if I am. Even if the doctor says I am. Insane people are only dreamers. They seem to think and reason in dream values. Because in dreams, even totally unrelated things make sense. Like this: A mystery dream about a hole cut in a desk to unlock the drawer and steal a cheap ring offers two possibilities. One (the one that I first figured out in the dream would be perfectly right) was that a strange "old friend" of my father's had quietly tagged behind him on a tour of the house, and while Father was in the next room, explaining some architecture plans, this man quickly felt the lock on the desk drawer and then followed Father. Fingerprints were taken later, when the hole was found cut in the desk and the ring taken. They matched the stranger's. But all of my detective work was rendered useless when I talked to a girl in an aquarium museum about it and she showed me the other alternative that turned out to be the answer in the end. She held up two starfish, as she called them, but I thought they looked more like angelfish. They both had beautiful blue fins with yellow stripes running horizontally. The one on the right's fin angled delicately to the right. The one of the left's tilted to the left. The latter was a freak. We concluded that the hole in the desk was no human crime, but rather caused by the freak starfish. It seemed to make sense. I was satisfied with it. Insanity is like that. And everyone is a little insane. Because we don't understand some people, we call them insane and lock them in hospitals or mental institutions where they can sometimes never be discharged. They can live out their "lives" (if you can call it that) "protected from themselves" with bars and locks and white walls and soft things. (Not too soft, of course, they might bury their heads and suffocate.) As a pass time, they are sent to "occupational therapy" to make purple leather wallets with plastic buck stiching and woven wicker baskets. Maybe, as a special treat, on holidays, they can all make decorations for their ward. Best of all — the times when they let them do their own thing, and you should see the beauty that results from it! I know. I worked in adult mental health in a local hospital for two years . . .

There were other times, walking down the hall and hearing all the feeble, terrified shouts, "Help me! Oh please, help!" coming from several rooms with closed doors. When I looked puzzled, a nurse came to me, seeing me standing in the hall, not knowing where to go first. "They're always like that," she said. "Leave them alone, there's nothing you can do."

One South was the convalescent unit, which, defined more clearly, was the place with the old people just waiting and wishing to die and leave the tubes and machines and drugs in the sterile world that kept them alive. Two South, on top of that, was the adult mental health. People walked around like zombies; sometimes I could even tell the ones that were taking the same drugs by their actions and reactions. Some shuffled, staring straight ahead with their arms hanging, and faces so vacant and pale that they looked inhuman.

I see people all saying, "help me"
I hear them every day
I hear them crying from the pain
and the long daylight.

What a place. I couldn't help but feel sorry and sometimes even frightened. It was a reality, that floor.

I had told a friend of mine who was contemplating suicide to first visit an infant ward, and see all the ugly, wrinkled-pink newborns that squirmed blindly in their sterile cribs. And then visit One South, the convalescents. She did, and it changed her mind . . . She looked at me and said, "I hadn't realized that life was so important to some people. I bet they spend thousands on hospital bills, the relatives of these people, just to keep them alive."

Insanity. Everyone is insane, really. Anyone different.

Getting into another topic, DRUGS. I'm crashing right now but when I started writing this I was pretty fucked up. I drew my interpretation of myself and used my little orange pupil-checker (mirror) for a basis. Then I drew the rest soley by what I felt like. Then I looked at it and said, "Wow, look at the spaced-out freak."

By the way, and for the record, I finally left at 1:30 after getting in here at 11:00. No, 10:30. Then I went into the can, forged a pass, and came right back in again. The last hour zipped so fast that when the bell rang at 2:25, I thought it was only 2:00.

There's this feeling I get when I see all the people at the "North Door" where everyone smokes. They all cram together for body heat and half of the time you end up face to face with some freak who puts his arm around you and says, "Keep me warm." It has been dubbed the corner drugstore now, as it is the largest pushing trade area in Mason county, yard for yard. Considering, of course, that there is only 12 by 12 feet of cement there, with 30 or 40 freaks on top of it. I bought 3 4-way blotter hits (acid) yesterday and 20 zips today, and people begin to look at you as the "burnout in the library" after awhile. They call me "Speed Queen," for god's sakes! Alright. I know it wrecks your mind, but that's my business. Again by society's standards, drugs are wrong. Here I go again, 5 more hits of zip and I'm on my way home. Something tells me I'm gonna be up for awhile.

November 14

5:39 and 39 seconds. Pulse . . . (oh jesus)

Interlude (quoted from the black diary)

"In so many books I've seen that are based on diaries, the subject is always found dead at the end and the diaries haven't been written in for a while before they die. That always happens . . .

"I've decided that I'm not making any sense anymore already. I've decided that I can't remember my past, just that I've been not myself. I've decided that speed is beautiful and acid is merely a mind-opener. And if, in fact, this is what I really believe, I'm as good as dead."

Friday, November 15

Three hundred and sixty five days ago today, Brendan started helping me. Today I felt very lonely. I went to the bowling alley. Brendan is away hunting.

"Why do you like the cops?" Because they care, in small ways; maybe [they have] legal interests, I don't know. They listen, because they might learn something that would be to their advantage. They're always there. They're someone that's there and they are safe. They usually don't change. In most cases.

"Why do you lie?"

Because I'm sad. I know no other way to let people know it. I want them to know it because I need a steady person to rap with.

"Do you think you've grown up any this past year?"

No, not really.

I should be sleeping in the yellow room at Sadie's now, thinking of tomorrow and of Brendan — I'm sleeping in my room which hasn't changed much, at least it still has red lights. And I am still very sad.

T.F.T.D. (Thoughts fuck this day.)

BRENDAN STILL HAS MY PEN . . . and I think I'm going to cry tonight.

Continued in blue notebook.

The zip has taken its toll now. What a relief. Now I can write again. That "internal alarm" that the Jesus freaks used to tell me about already went off, but I took them anyway. I don't worry too much, I know God will forgive me. He must wonder why I wear this crucifix around my neck at all sometimes. I can't explain it. I know I don't need it (the zip), but I take it anyway. Why is it? Rebellion, maybe. A sense of being able to think more clearly, write faster, be feeling pretty mellow and happy and high. Wow, though. My hand under the candle is so intricate. This is the third time only that I've taken real zip, and I'm scared already. What's worse is the thing I'm scared of: not being able to find any more zip. Now, though, I can get off it anytime with God's help. I must be a real God-user. And how I used to tell everyone I was doing dope! Hell, I didn't even know what white cross looked like. I thought speed was always shot up. I thought acid was only in sugar cubes. I knew it was a game at first, but I had myself believing I was addicted. What can start out as a game can end in death. I have to face that now, before it's too late. I see a fork in the road and last year when it all started, it was way ahead of me, and I wasn't worried. I had a straight road for awhile, built on tricks for getting attention from authority, built on games for getting love . . . I remember that road, although it wasn't totally forgotten all this time, but now I look at it and it's splitting right under my feet.

Cry on your own shoulder

Jefferson Airplane must be spaced. As I was saying . . . I know I've had that feeling of living two lives:

Life No. 1: the one I started with. The one that seemed to be my own, but I can't tell anymore. Horses, school, good grades, thinking — good thinking — and writing. Writing for others, not just myself. Caring, baby-sitting, working at the hospital. Straight friends, rowdy but not destructive. Interested in my future, in a people-helping job. Satisfied with my life, never giving up. Realizing my games as games and my lies as lies. With the desire to love and be loved, to take care of people, talk to them because I know what it's like to be alone. Letting my voice tell sad people everything would be alright.

Life No. 2: The one I'm still wondering who started. Freaks are my main friends. Taking the horse out at night. Failing school. Insanity, dreaming, shrinks. [Thoughts about] foster homes, pigs, zip. Destructive and loving it. Hiding, running, no communication unless I'm high, cool, unfeeling, sly to get by, stealing drugs from the hospital, afraid of babies, don't give a shit about tomorrow (except for getting more dope). Not knowing how to handle the main two extremes of people [burnout and straight]. Losing friends as they move out and go their own ways.

I still partially respect the pigs, realize that most pigs are pigs and sometimes O.K. people. It's really the smart-ass Dick Tracy pigs that degrade the force. I am doubtful of any cop that seems friendly now. Maybe he would be a good friend, but I just can't risk a pocket full of zip for a friend. I will admit, there was one that was like a brother to me for awhile. He gave me places to go for help with my family, and he listened (even though he might have been eating or drinking coffee at the same time, he listened). I could trust him for awhile, and I should have thanked him then because he deserved it, but it was too hard to say thank you then, too . . . When you're my age, you gotta know it's risky as hell to have a cop for a friend. Last year all the kids in the class thought I was a narc. Holy shit, what a joke. This year I've learned not to talk about it at all. It's risky for the poor pig to have a freak for a friend, too. Like, "Look, Henry, what's that girl doing in the front seat of that squad car in that empty parking lot? I'm going to report this."

"Such a disgrace. Tch, tch, tch."

I got off the track there for sure. Continuing: I have no outlook at all, always expecting a disaster and not too sure if I can take it. Looking for a shoulder to cry on, and a back to split the weight, among the burnies and strung-out minds that always tell each other everything's alright, when they know that it isn't and may not be for a long, long time.

There's obviously something to this comparison. My first life person would be an almost perfect companion for the second life person. The fixer and the hopeless case. But it's hard to cry on your own shoulder, although I have frequently told myself everything's alright. Except for the burnies, no one else ever tells me it is. Probably because it's NOT alright after all. But I know that. Right now I'm at an unhappy compromise. I don't know who God planned me to be. I still consider myself a Christain in both lives, it's just that I'm a good Christain in the first life, and in the second — shall I use a familiar term? — borderline passing.

Hold up there, Queen. You know why you call yourself a Christain? Because you're scared shitless.

I enjoy trips into my mind. Sometimes they scare me. When I'm zipping, emotions come pouring out of me. All unrelated and stinking because they've been in there for so long. Did you know emotions stink? If meat is kept out it spoils. Like that. They frequently get screwed up and twisted around so that they make absolutely no sense. But even that's cool. They get the hell out of my packed brain for awhile. I can write with more gusto and faster, not only because my hand's receiving all the zip, but my thoughts come faster and I have to keep up with them. One problem is that I get off the track a lot. And I can't continue to write in this notebook unless I'm stoned because my burnt values are different from my straight values. (The way it goes, one part of you is more full of shit than the other, and after you get good and burnt, they kind of blend together until you don't know what you're talking about and you're COMPLETELY full of shit.) Like I said, "I love people?" I do? I don't know what prompted me to say that. I think I do. Maybe I don't. It depends. None of the above.

Now I'm starting to crash again and my writer's bump has a charlie horse. My neck is locked down and to the right. My gut feels like a towel being rung out. I wonder if speed queens get immune to that strycnine? I mean shit. Well no, I don't mean shit. I mean really. If the factories are going to be cheap about it, why don't they just use powdered milk or something? This strycnine cycle is bound to knock off a few in town before it's done circulating. Blotter acid costs about 2 cent a hit to make. They rip us off for a buck fifty a hit. It's late. I've been writing since 10:30 this morning and now it's 10:23. Pulse 90, I'm crashed.

Conversation with the Queen

I are here again. Took another five. Pulse 78 and rising. Flew last night. Didn't sleep for five minutes. Fear, I think. After five more — "That makes it 10 today," Alice said wearily with snap fire in her eyes. They were clearly pin-point and danced when she blinked. There was a most perfect devil's halo surrounding the tiny pupils.

"Yes," laughed the Cheshire cat, hanging ominously from an oak limb. She watched him and his smile stayed, the rest of him was off somewhere. (And she knew, too, that Cheshire cats don't eat mice; however, they do accept advice from them now and then, and that was a relief.)

"Follow your head," they said. "It takes you where you should not go, while dining on your dreams." (And she knew it wasn't a teaparty.)

"Keep your head," said the head that listened to the stereo through encyclopedias. And the other surely said, "Feed your head," while totally engulfed in the talking bookshelves (although it didn't bother him). Speed Queen, Soani, Mary Jane, Chains, Machine Gunn, Muff, Narc (ha) . . . Who?

"Know what I found out?"

"What did you find out?"

"Iron Butterfly . . . "

"Who?"

"Can't fly too good with a name like that."

"I agree . . . anyway, they wrote Inna Gadda Da Vida, right?"

"Definately." (Can't spell too good anymore, gotta watch yourself, Queen.)

"What do you think about Kevin's suggestion?"

"Oh, well, I think it's stupid as hell. You're out to have fun, right?"

"Right!"

"Then why get serious?"

"Hmmm . . . well, I won't hear you, you know. I don't have to."

"One wrong move from you and I'll have you in the ground. You know that."

"Don't . . . let's not have another fight, Queen?" (Why the "?" Who knows?)

"Are you going to give in?"

"I can't. How could I?"

"Yes, that's right. I'm the mother here. I know that. So why the lecture? Why the question in the first place?"

"I'm sorry. You upset me sometimes. You can be mean, you know."

"That's the way I am and I have no human feelings."

"My feelings are based on chemicals. If I'm down and I like it, that's cool. If I want an up, I take an up. If I am empty (and I hate to be empty) I take a trip. If I want to sleep, I take a down. It's nice being able to control your body."

"Good going, kid. Want me to say it? It's about time now. It's alright. Everything is . . ."

• • •

"Queen, you look awful."

"Thanks and I know. How awful?"

"Kind of green, maybe a little gray."

"Oh. That's cool."

"It's alright then?"

"I ain't worried."

"Good. It doesn't pay. Nothing does . . ."

"Well, yeah, I know."

"Pushing it."

"Definitely."

"You got it this time, Queen."

"Uh huh . . . know what?"

"Probably, but shoot."

"You were seeing things last night."

"I understand."

"Sure you do. I'll make you understand everything. Just keep going. Feed your head."

"Did he really say that?"

"I don't know but he thought it. Definitely."

"Well, I thought that before he said, 'Keep your head.' That is more of an 'it's alright' sentence in that song. I think it needs that. It's comforting."

• • •

"They're really ugly. But people love them."

"Who are you speaking of?"

"Babies, of course. But it applies to a majority of things."

"Burnies, too?"

"Yes, dear."

"Even Queens?"

"Even the royal Queen herself."

"Do you think yourself ugly, Queen?"

"I don't know. Candles form me beautifully. But white lights . . ."

"Yes, I know."

"Well, what are you seeing?"

"My future."

"What else?"

"My past."

"Is that cool?"

"And my present."

"Oh . . . I bet you feel pretty bad, huh? I can fix that."

"How? Oh yeah. An up arrow. More again. Don't you ever feel guilty?"

She tries to look sorry. "I don't know. It's maybe been burnt away. Do you ever feel your head is a beautiful flaming fire bursting with thoughts and wild dreams . . . and then suddenly you have to stand back from yourself and cover your eyes at the intensity . . . and then you have to hold your breath and jump right back in to make sure you gather yourself in again as the fire dies?"

"Yes. I've felt that when thinking on your level."

"You mean flying at my height?"

"Yes, I guess that's it."

"Have you noticed that it's like watching embers in a

fireplace? Eventually they flicker to ashes and smoke and die and you get cold again?"

"Yes, Queen. And that's where I sometimes try to talk you out of it, but you come back again anyway and you're always there."

"But you can't possibly want us dead?"

"What do you mean, Queen?"

"If I die, I can bring you with me. Or I can wait, but I'll still be there, in some form. And you won't know me. You'll think I'm dead and gone. Then . . . I'll attack, and you'll be with me again wherever I go forever because the last time . . . that one last time (as you will call it) . . . will never end. I won't let you go then. I have you, dear."

"I know."

"But if I catch you thinking about 'one more time' and I think you're serious, I'll take you for my own. Because I know you don't want to turn to ashes and smoke and be cold like the dead fire. You can't tell. When the fire is dying, sometimes they go with it. The freaks, I mean. Most of them get scared of the risk and do zip again, refuel the fire. Each time it will take more kindling to get it going. And when it does finally die, it will not be relit again. Not ever. Understand?"

"Yes, I think so."

"You don't, but I'll make you, sooner or later. Don't worry now. It's alright," she said, leaving me with firewood and some bared fears of burning. "It's alright," she said, and then she was gone. I wonder if it's by my will that she left? Do you think I still have control over her?

"Yes, Queen . . . yes, I'm coming."

I went out around by the North Door again, and trucked behind the hill to make a zip exchange with some little kid. I was all nervous and shakey, for some damned reason, and he had to count it out for me. It seems ironic that I've gotten so much money and gotten away with getting it. This morning it was cold and all kind of a purple or black-light winter before sunrise and I passed the neighbor kids who were waiting for the bus. I looked down and felt lower than a boot heel. Must have been a good 30 below and it was the kind of weather where I had to wrap my long antique fur coat tight around me to hold the warmth in. I had no money and no zip. Totally bankrupt. Mike's service station at the corner cashed me a ten dollar check. I went on. Got to school and the hall floors were wet and muddy. Big deal. So what else is there to write about? It was the same as it has been for days. Seemingly years. Straight to the fresh morning dope deals at the North Door. All the dope was still being sought out in town by my main speed pusher. Spaceman fronted me five until the time that he got back. There was a bunch of little junkie brats practically knee high to me that were forking out money and waiting for Spaceman's return. So I told them I had all the zip that day but had to wait to make sure I couldn't sell it all in a large quantity of 500 to an "interested person" all at once. They flocked around me like baby ducks for what was left of the morning, and I shook them off long enough to meet Spaceman at the North Door. He only had a hundred, so I took my ten and got enough to last me maybe two days — 50. The ducks found me again, and I delighted in telling their pouting faces that I had sold 450 and wanted the rest for lunch. That was really what I was today. Out to lunch. High, down there! (Quack.)

Alright, whoever you are. Get together now, kid. Pull it up and around. That's right. You almost didn't come back there for a minute. You scare me sometimes. "Beware of darkness, it can hit you, it can hurt you, make you sore and what is more . . . that is not what you are here for" (George Harrison special). Maybe . . . no, Queen left for now. She has a lot of people to talk to. Different ones than *you* can talk with, right, Narc?

Yes. Complete opposites. But they were my companions at one time? (Again "?" This is screwed.)

Do you think Kevin is trying to trick you?

No, I know that it is not all that bad. I've been busted before. It hurts. Yes, if they care, it hurts. I don't want them to be afraid of me or mad at me for being at the North Door. I don't belong anywhere else.

I am the part of you that gets high, and gets busted, then there is also the part of you who still keeps the old friends from straight days, the pigs.

I am torn, because they were the only real friends when I was lonely, yet what they ask me to do for them now is to narc on the friends that have kept me safe from cruel reality. How can I help both, living the way I do? I agree with the police in my first life, but my second life person doesn't quite dig that. Because I've had week-ends when I was without junk. Didn't bother me when I was in between (and more into my first person a bit), but things have really changed.

I just can't believe it. I can't believe it's finally happened to me, all this. After watching Tom totally drift away the same way, and being unfeeling, maybe not knowing just what to feel. Too bad we weren't together through all of it. If we both lived through it, we could have converted together too. Might have made us closer. Why didn't that teach me anything? WHY? It is absolutely igorant to do what I'm doing. Tom . . . was also once like I am now. I don't want to go through with all that. I don't want to scale fences or be locked in rooms or be busted, I don't want to hurt Dad & Mom. I just can't hurt them.

Here's a thought. Picture your parents both killed in an auto accident. Would it change your life suddenly? O.K. I'm at school a week after the funerals for the first time since the accident. Now. How do I feel? I'm sitting in the library, where I am, actually, and what am I thinking? What will I do? Screw-up because they're not around to protect me anymore? Or change just for them? Is there a medium way? . . . I'd have some choices, and right now I only know what they are, not which ones I'd take.

1. Stop living back when the accident happened — just live in the past, afraid of the future.
2. Get so burnt I wouldn't know who I was. Now I don't want that because I am fairly religious and I believe that writing and understanding human situations is God's gift to me, personally.
3. Turn whole heartedly to Christianity.
4. Run away; foster home or hospital.
5. End my career with horses, not being able to support them.
6. Kill someone.
7. Kill myself.
8. Hide inside my brain and let it take me.
9. Pray for my life —

Or if Tom went with them? — Wow, I can't think of that at all. It's too scarey.

• • •

"Hi."

"Hello."

"I haven't heard from you for quite a while."

"So?"

"I'm afraid to ask you what you're here for, Soani."

"Then you don't have to know."

"But don't say anything more, Soani. Your voice is like a sword. Why?"

"Why did you destroy the altar? Why are you giving in to these Christains? Can't you see Kevin is tricking you?"

"Well, he is different . . ."

"So were the others."

She left. Pulse 108 again. Help, oh shit. Don't help, but don't leave me alone. Get away from my life, no . . . exist with me . . . Joella, where are you? I know that you are around. I last saw you in the flame . . .Here I am again in front of it . . . but you're not there . . . You're dead and gone and it was years ago but I can't forget . . .

Shit. This isn't funny. I can't write a blessed thing in here unless I'm flyin'.

• • •

I didn't believe the Jesus freaks' scare tactics. But it all fits. Sleepless nights, days without food, euphoria, super depression. I must be crashed now. I really fell hard that time. I think maybe I will fall harder tomorrow, though. Everyday is harder and I can feel it still. It's like a rope pulling me in. I'm scared, but still curious . . . or really, well, I don't know what it is exactly, but I still take the junk anyway. No, it's not curiosity. That's been satisfied. It's that desire to write something so deep and meaningful. Because if I let go of my writing, I become just another junkie on the streets with nothing, I let go of the only thing I have. It's so far out because I can write so fast and not remember what I said two sentences back. I can read it then, and see how much sense it makes, and it's like I've never seen it before. Like someone else wrote it all. It's good reading until you reach the part where I'm crashed. Then nothing is so meaningful at all anymore and you wonder if everything else that you've ever written is worth the painful coming down hard and hitting bottom. It sounds . . . well, not normal anymore, but like someone else. Another mind. Anyone's but mine. And really screw that. Super screw that. I'm moving so slow now. I can't stand it. My body's aching but my head's on fire. My muscles won't stop working even at night. I feel so damn low. Almost through the earth now. Think of it now. I lost myself again.

"Queen, how had you known I was here?"

"I could feel it. You sound crashed."

"I am, I think."

"When did you first start it all? It seems you've been like that all your life."

"No, that's just the zip working."

"It's just that you can't remember."

"Yes, I can."

"Definitely you can. Try it once. Last Monday night . . . what did you have for dinner?"

"Nothing."

"Well, O.K. You got me. Remember the fire?"

"It's hard to put it out of my mind, Queen. I've been thinking . . ."

"The hell you have, don't you see? You just fly. You don't really think. Not after you get started. You lose all your feelings after awhile. But you can learn to control them, too. It's not that they're totally gone, or anything . . . you just can't tell what's causing them ever. The zip or the real person you are. Or were, I guess. No one's really real anymore either. They all play games at some time."

"Yes, I know . . ."

"LOOK UP!" she said suddenly and was gone before I could . . .

"Queen? Queen?"

Above me perched the Cheshire cat, this time bringing his tree along . . . and I stared and he stared and I watched the smile curve slyly down to his chin and up to his whiskers. "Take a rat to lunch," he said with a surprisingly authorative tone of voice.

"You look like Hubert," I said, but was glad when I realized I'd only thought it.

I didn't sleep at all last night. That damn pig radio. It was on again to keep me company and it seems different cars got their audios at different levels. They were all quiet and mellow and I was nearing a cat nap when who but Hubert should have his audio way the hell up and practically shoot me through the ceiling. I wasn't making much sense then — (there's something creaking outside my door) — but I recall leaning over and saying something like, "Shhh, you'll wake up my parents." Right to the radio.

About this time I start getting bored of getting high and sitting on my butt all day, but there's nothing else to do. I want to be who I am, but I don't know just who that is. I hope I die or go nuts because it would be easier than getting together what I've pushed apart.

I see a train comin!
There ain't no tracks.
I got this feeling that I won't be comin' back.
There may be sunshine and there may be rain,
I'll never feel 'em if I'm blinded by pain.
I'm hearing whistles from a non-existant train . . .
I see a railroad bridge that's rotted and worn,
Felt the wheels for ages, now the tracks have been torn.
There is a chance that for me it will hold
If people ask me — well, I never was told,
but standing in the middle,
I'm not quite as bold . . .

Secondary mindpicking with the Queen

Hey, I'm here again, I think. Maybe a little less than before, but I am here. I bought 30, but they're raunchy ones. Just so they have that salty, sour taste going down. God, I'm depressed. I guess it *is* like they say: The more you get high, the more you get burnt, the more you get burnt, the less you make sense, the less you make sense, the more useless you feel, the more you feel useless, the more depressed you get, and the more depressed you feel, the more you get high, the more you get high, the more you raise your doses, the more you raise your doses, the more useless you become. It could go on, but it ends with death. I can pull out now, but I keep thinking I'll have time later. I'll still be able to, without outside help.

That must be the Queen again. Must be.

"Know what?"

"What now?"

"I talked to Roy last night. Aren't you paranoid?"

"I should be. But I'm not yet. He won't bust me unless I give him the chance."

"You probably already have . . ."

"Maybe. I just don't think he wants to bust me."

"You can't tell."

"No . . . you never can anymore. People are so fucking different. They'll tell you things; some mean them, some don't. They'll make promises. Some keep them, some don't. The ticket is to learn to read people. Look right at them hard. See how they react. Stand inside their closeness boundaries. There are ways to do it, you know."

"Yes, I guess. Do you read people?"

"All the time."

"What do you do with what you gather and conclude about them?"

"I don't conclude anything. I merely gather data. If I'm interested, I'll try to put it all together."

"But what then? You can't label people when you're not sure at all of who they really are. They could be playing games that cover their real selves. And if they are, they are hiding for a definite reason. They're either afraid to open themselves to others, or they don't like themselves, or their real selves don't fit in with the people they're trying to impress. But only a real self has a conscience. Only the real self can say, I know this is wrong, but I don't care. Only a real self can actually care at all. Game players aren't all bad. There is always a reason for it, depending on the game. The games are usually based on self-esteem (ego) and the people they're trying to impress. A combination of those. Understand?"

"I think so, yes. There are a few I know . . . I'm sure of it, Queen."

"Name them."

"Well, there's quite a lot that play the spacey and thoughtful game. They try to base it on drugs. Most of them are fairly straight. They play insane, although some do dream a lot . . . and being insane is a safe thing. People take care of you, lock you in at night . . . and you can say anything or do anything to them without a care because they know it's not your fault that you're that way. Like you don't have any conscience or values at all. And maybe if you *try* to be crazy when you're not, maybe then you lose your values. You're insane to want to be insane when you have a well-in-order head."

"You think that, really?"

"I said it, that's all I know. I get to rambling after a while."

"Yeah, me too."

"Are you flying, Queen?"

"Yes, but it's not quite as good a feeling as it used to be."

"You noticed that, too?"

"Yes, very much so. I'm very depressed."

"That's what it's doing to you, Queen."

"No, no . . . remember it's alright . . . "

"But you know it's not really."

"But of course it is. It has to be because there is nothing else."

"What do you mean?"

"I don't know. I really don't know."

"Did you once?"

"I can't remember."

"Yeah, I'm that way too. Why do you think so low of yourself? Oh, ha, you've heard that question, too."

"Yes, I was there, but I tried to stay out of the conversation."

"Very good. But why do I — I mean you — really?"

"You think I do?"

"Yes . . ."

"How can you tell?"

"It really shows, Queen. People that think low of themselves, really, and no bulltweed, are generally quite self-destructive."

"I am?"

"Well, you are a little greener than yesterday . . . You're just not . . . well, there's something missing."

"I only want to find out who I really am. That's all. You can't criticize me for that."

"Well, I can, but it's harder on you, so I won't. But I'm still at the point where I know it's wrong. Because, yes. I was depressed before. And yes, I'm depressed now still. So it didn't do anything helpful for me at all, did it?"

"You met me."

"Yes, I did, didn't I? The person that I've been playing as a role for a long time. Wow . . . another breakthrough."

"What's it now?"

"See, when I used to pretend to be the big drug user, the lonely scared addict who needed people to talk to but didn't know how to really get to them, I was lying. And people went along with me for a while. It worked. Slowly I made mistakes and people got to catching them and they thoroughly put me away and rejected me for it. Maybe I'm just going back and doing it all over again. To punish myself for what I did. It does seem a fit way to die in that sense. Be straight and lie that you're burnt, and be really burnt and lie that you're straight and . . . like both of us, Queen, always say it's alright, hold tight. And then people pass you by and don't pay you any special attention at all, because you *say* you're happy. And they don't realize what you're doing until it's too late."

"Yes, that's true, maybe."

"And something more before I lose it . . . Comparing Tom and me, I know I started "messing up" when I *played* the junkie. In school and everywhere. Right? Oh, wow, it's just such a complete and perfect cross. People just didn't notice."

"What are you rambling about?"

"I'm only trying to make sense out of something. Now I may have found something to go on . . . Now, at home and with old friends, I'm either playing straight and happy with no complaints, or I'm conforming to their standards . . . their ideas of who I really am. They're all individual. I have to play a different role for each of them to satisfy them . . . that I'm O.K. and nice and a good friend. I form myself to their values so they'll like me better. It's hard to relate on their level when you're not really on their level at all, understand?"

"Well, not really."

"Now, a year after I pretended to be the way I am now, I am the way I pretended to be then. Only a lot more scared, a lot more feeling that there are no games here. I know it's real. I hate it because after I lost that first person playing that game, he's not about to believe me now or offer me any help that he was giving me when I didn't really need it. I made him feel foolish. He lends an ear, talks to me seriously, gives me advice . . . and then realizes it's really all been for nothing. But I wonder if Tom started that way? I think he did. All for attention, too, but refusing to admit it. But they didn't believe him at first, and to show them, he played insane and used drugs to help him. That way, he almost did go insane and he got the whole treatment. Police, the hospital, drug programs, etc. And the parents treated him bad. They didn't try to, they just thought they were helping. They yelled, never seemed to just talk to him. And he got revenge. More drugs. More police. More trouble. Ha, ha, ha. You can't control me anymore, see? I'm on my own and I'm going wherever. And you can't stop me. How does that feel? They didn't want to believe it. Their own kid! For a while it was "a phase." Then it turned out to be a "problem" (when he was half dead). And now they say, 'Well, it damaged his brain, you know.' Like it had always been that way. So with me it's different. It's like trying to chase something that won't run. I don't fight back. I just sit there and take it. By the Bible, that's right. Psychologically it can kill you. Just keeping it inside. Because it's not that I don't get mad. I seem to relate their fury to those fights with Tom, not me at all. It's not a case of what I'm doing to them, it's a case of what I'm doing to myself. And the rest of my life. Did I lose you, Queen?"

"ZZZZZZZZZZZZZZZZZZZZZ."

"Well, I guess I don't blame you. It doesn't involve you at all."

"Huh, but . . ."

"You think it does, Queen?"

"Well, I really . . . no, no, of course it doesn't. It's alright. Well, then, goodnight."

"Good-night, Queen. Don't sleep too long. You may lose yourself in dreaming."

END

There's something about that library. Oh, screw it. I don't really want to write this. But I don't have anything else anymore. Screw it anyway. It stinks. I think . . . no, screw that, too . . . I don't think anymore really. Anyway, I'm very, very tired. Yesterday I called Gracie the cat "Queen." And yesterday the bus passed Queens Lane (anyone who takes the sure road is as good as dead . . . [was that] Carl Jung?). And my next sight-halt was a sign by a church. "Peace be with you," it said quietly, with a dove. That's about the all of it, I guess. See, at first I was saying to myself, "Get high, go ahead . . . just remember to stop when the going gets heavy." And I said it every time after I took off and I said it again. "Don't worry. I'll be able to tell when I'm out of touch with reality." But there was no way, because I was stoned all the time. I fell hard just this morning. Really crashed. But I bought more during lunch, 100 of them. And again I was off. Slowed a little. That stock was really cheap.

And then I said, "No. What's happened is that I've finally come to admitting that I'm not about to stop now." And then I thought a little, or tried. And all at once once something came down on me and really had me on the floor.

I guess I didn't realize that I'd been out of touch with reality long before I got around to ever thinking the going might be getting just a little rough. And now it's too late. I'm gone. You just don't think about things like that when you're up. It's like you have only a little time to be in that state of mind and a lot to cover during it. And when you're up so much that you can't tell whether you're high or not half the time, then you're out of touch with reality.

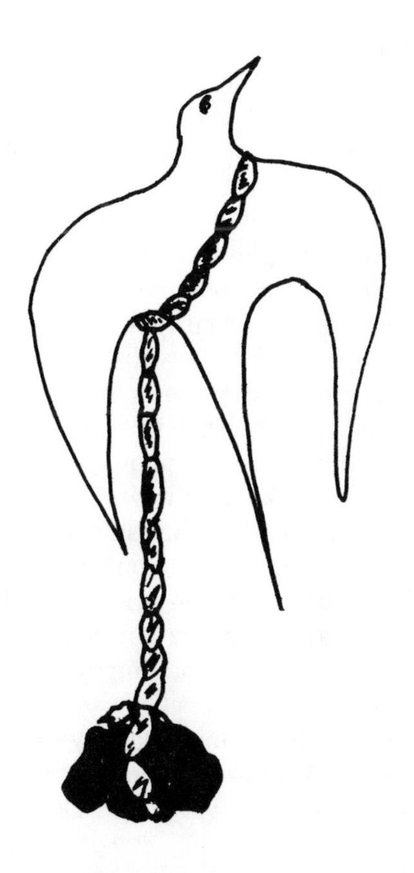

When are you going to choose?

November 22, Friday

"It's all right (not really)."

What kills me about the photograph I'm looking at is that it's me; complete in a symbolic way, revealing who I am now. But it's me when I was maybe 10. Oh, God, only five years ago . . . Take those five years and try to imagine the learning involved in them; interpretation of emotions, putting them into words, people, events, changes. Wow. But it's all there, really. The radio with the upward antenna . . . the model riding stable with the roof displaced, a box I used for pencils, scissors and crayons for drawing and writing and making things, another stable I made from a Gainesburger box and painted, turtle bowl and food. Messy and disorganized atmosphere, the open desk piled with papers, the chair at the table with the radio, the box beneath it. Two windows, one with curtains closed and one with curtains slightly opened. White walls, and the gold frame that still hangs at the same place holding a photograph of Tom. (Mine was either not up yet, or just out of the picture.) The curtains themselves are of opaque white lace. And me staring with the same look I have now sometimes. Very hard for me to interpret. It could be slightly aggressive, annoyed, or disliking the intrusion of the camera into my youthful privacy. Maybe a little fearful in a way (maybe just that I *should* have been, knowing my future). Thoughtful and silent, and a little dreamy . . . holding my feelings in then, too. I can see it in my face.

Really, a young version of my life five years later . . . that is, now. The radio I have now is similar, but is usually on the police band, but if I'm rowdy, on KDON. (This one in the picture was stolen out of my father's office not long after this.)

The misplaced stable roof symbolizes horses, of course, and the fairly disorganized way I've always been about them. The cardboard stable symbolizes the makeshift horse-life I live sometimes, trying to use what I already have to save money for new equipment. The pencil box I have now is enlarged somewhat, but I still have one. When I'm sitting in the type of environment where I can express an idea on paper, I always have what I need . . . paper, a vague or definite feeling or thought in my mind, and a pencil. The environment here is an identical one to my present. But it seems more relaxed.

The open desk drawer with the pile of paper is self-explanatory. The white walls — getting deeper into symbolism — depicts youth, future, life . . .

And the windows in the wall . . . one with curtains closed, one open. It is both dark and empty through them. Seems a choice which I'm facing now, which window to climb through? I'm not really sure which one means previously mentioned Life No. 1 and Life No. 2. It depends on how you feel about each of these lives. Life No. 1 could be the closed window, in that it is fairly safe and healthy and standard (knowing what to expect). Or it could be Life No. 2; standing before it you can only see so far, and the curtains block the rest, meaning that that kind of life ends with a misfortune . . . either death or insanity sooner or later. Before you realize that you can't or haven't been seeing all that was really there, and then it's too late.

Or standing behind it and looking in (the room symbolizing life) and seeing it blurry and hideous and with no pathway to return to it on . . . opaqueness to life that enables you to hide from reality by not understanding it (not seeing it).

The second window can also be either. Life No. 1 in the sense that it's open and easy to get to, sure and confident. The darkness outside meaning the always unknown future, in this case, not feared at all. Or Life No. 2, revealing an open mind, a new road, deep thoughts, through endless darkness, lighting the way with drugs and held-in emotions. In a way, it seems that the window on the right and the window on the left can both be climbed through, and right now the one on the right seems to have an easier future. It all depends on which life I'm living when I think about it. I wonder if you can tell from this interpretation which life I'm in now? The Second, of course . . . but somehow regretfully. Longing to be happy again and able to live with my interests . . . all of them at once like I did then.

And on the wall in the center, the young picture of Tom hiding his head in a black hat. It's still there. The hat he was wearing he picked up somewhere, but for my picture, my mother made me one — red velvet with flowers, considered quite queenly at the time. I can't quite tell if the fact that the picture appears to be hanging nearer to the left window than the right means anything, because it only appears to be. Actually the wall is angled, half of a bay window, and the curtains on the left are covering the window frame. So the picture is hanging centered . . . like he was, all the time (I know that because he's still alive and smart). But until people move that curtain, or the picture itself, he appears unsure. He is also on the white wall, meaning youth, but closer to it than it was then, facing the windows and only looking through them. Not yet desiding if he should, in fact, climb through either.

It seems fairly obvious that I am the subject of the picture, but the first thing that I notice is myself and the radio. The most familiar to others, too, because everyone knows what a radio and a person look like. The picture carries a strange feeling that I can't understand. But I wonder sometimes if I know what the feeling is after all. And in the picture, I'm saying two things, "Here I am where I'm supposed to be, and going alright so far, but I want it to be my decision which way I go, when I go. As yet, I haven't the care to even look through the window. The choices aren't apparent to me." Or, "What the hell do you expect me to do with a choice like this all by myself?"

And fear. That picture speaks so loud to me that it's practically screaming. THERE YOU WERE THEN, HERE YOU ARE NOW . . . WHERE ARE YOU GOING TO GO? WHEN ARE YOU GOING TO CHOOSE?"

The eye you can't see cries the biggest tear

Sunday, November 24

I went to the bowling alley today, and Hubert came up in his new pickup truck and Brendan came up in the new squad car. So big deal. All that makes us realize is that they're still alive. Two old "ladies" were talking behind us . . . "Look at that . . . those officers with those young ladies . . . isn't that revolting?" Screw 'em. Sadie left, of course, without saying thankyou or anything (Hubert bought her lunch). But big deal, I can't let it bring me down, I've got enough bringing me down without year-old paraphrenalia in there with it, too. So it happened today. Same thing could have been last year. That's got to be all dead now. Screw this. I'm lying here in bed not wanting to move my buns in the least bit but then wondering why I'm wasting a good Saturday night. Probably because suicidal people could really give a shit. I don't know anything for absolutely certain. I mean, yeah, I'm alive. But only alive by society's rules. By the standards of a medical doctor. But then why should a medical doctor have standards and what the hell are standards anyway? Or for that matter, what is a medical doctor? There's probably a definition. Bullshit, that's all. Or why the hell is the sky blue? Oh, screw that explanation. I feel like stone river. Simon hasn't called or anything. Screw Mom, too. He's not a "confused man," he's a human being, if that's an accomplishment. He's alive. He can see, speak, hear, walk, etc. But not really. Not by *my* standards. But screw my standards. He is lonely, scared, and he wants somebody. I have to decide whether I can risk my life or my reputation, or maybe just my emotion on him. I know he's unpredictable. But I can't lose him again because there's too much there.

Monday morning the 25th of November, and the day is just a few minutes new. Friday I had no hope and I almost wished I still had school so I could sit in the library at least. I felt too low to get high, I felt useless and ignorant, and guilty. When I finally decided that I was sorry, I prayed for a good, long time and went home on the early bus. I rode, feeling the brunt of the long, bummer weekend ahead.

I saw Shelly at Big Mike's sandwich shoppe, and talked for awhile. Mom tried to get me to go to Christian Life. She's nuts. I went home and watched Perry Mason about some junkies. Stash, Ray, Margo and I trucked. I ditched my baby (zip bottle) under some leaves behind the bushes so I could get rowdy and destructive without my speed falling into the hands of the pigs. I found Zombie (from school) and a friend and the whole herd of us went to a party behind the boat works. I still hate parties because no one knows anyone but they pretend they do so they won't feel so lonely. I stood alone by a tree and watched for pigs. Under the dim light of the house, the unmarked cruised without lights like a shark waiting for the kill. "Pig!" I yelled, but they didn't listen so I left and sat on the bridge over the canal. As I left, another pig pulled in. Damned if I could find anyone that I came with, and damned if they cared, either.

I passed the gas station and some little kids pulled out a knife and cut an air hose. Further along, there was a fight at the theatre, and as I neared highway 13 off of County Road X, a man walked across the road with a cane, a top hat, and a tux. Some freaks asked me if I wanted to go to Alaska with them. I met Artful Dodger and he introduced me to Dan. We trucked until late. Home, bed.

The blacksmith came and shod both horses. Then Sadie and Cherries came. Seiche, Spatts and the colt all went out to the pasture. Spatts cantered for the first time since he broke his leg. I went to Cherries' for the night. We called Hubert the pig and apologized for being a couple of smartasses. "Granted," he says.

Woke up. To the bowling alley with my camera. Sadie, me, Cherries, Mom, Turd, Artful Dodger, and Tom all hauled hay for winter. It looked as if it would snow. Picked up the colt's papers. I went up to Big Mike's and trucked. I was stoned on 20. I went in to have coffee (as if I needed it) with my pig buddy, Roy. And my god, there was Simon. We buzzed around for awhile. He is still spacey. Goodnight. Feels like it's been just one long day.

Mon., Nov. 25

Only eleven today (zips). Dan came over and hid in the closet.

Could a radio pick up electric fence batteries? Well, they do because Brendan just buzzed and so did the dispatcher. Should I ask Seiche to unplug it? It's pretty ridiculous because he'd probably unplug the wrong one and get an electric schnookie. I can see it now in neon!

First electric riding all-season combination mud-plower, ice-melter, lawn-mower, trail-clearer, battery-charger . . .

Or, Coming Soon, *The Horse with the Electric Schnookie!* — rated PG.

> I just met two friends that I know were stoned.
> One was smilin' and flappin' like a sparrow.
> One was reelin' and rollin' and ramblin'.
> One was flyin' and flippin' and floorin'.

The tripper, the flipper, and the zipper. We got to talking about Spaceman [a name for a local pusher] and someone said he was drafted. What a bummer. He's either dead or halfway there because spacemen can't tolerate death. Well, I never knew him too well, if at all, and there wasn't much of him to salvage even so. And then we asked about god, and someone asked if anyone knew what had become of him. We shook our heads. Of course, this wasn't the big "G", God, it's just the little guy at the North Door that pushes anything that can change your head in the slightest to things that can push it too far and not let it come back. That's probably where he is himself. Some guy came in yesterday and someone says, "Hey, what are you doin' out of jail?" He didn't say anything.

So much for that. The one that was reelin' kept backing into me all the time and I knew I'd seen him somewhere before. Maybe not. But the silent guy. I knew him. From the yard party in Spring Valley last year. He was the dude with the glassy eyes.

This sets me up, doing all of this. It makes me happy, just writing. If you're high, it's about the only constructive thing to do. But what I'm missing is the destructive thing that's so hard to perceive sometimes. That's worded wrong. I'm being destructive by missing what I'm missing. A chance, maybe, that's all. I can't remember a whole day in school anymore. I don't believe there was a whole week ever when I went every day. It might be the fact that I've got a mental block like an iron wall about learning since last year. All of a sudden comes Algebra and BANG. I was thinking and dreaming, because I didn't like it at all and I only wanted to get it over with. Especially after the operation. My ankle hurt and it even hemoraged sometimes. But there sat Mrs. Williams, busy and quick and snappy, scrawling out what could make no sense at all and I wondered why anyone would want to make sense of it anyway. I realized I was slipping. Same Algebra book this year, too. I always have the feeling that people that are happy are living Life No. 1's. I'm late and behind all the people my age that I was right up there with until last year. And even though I didn't know anyone this year, they were all still ahead of me somehow. The ones that never had notebook paper and came to the class and slept were better than me. They had to be better. They were at least there and I wasn't. I was physically there, drifting in and out of my mind. There I remained until I was totally gone. Then I figured, what the hell. Goodbye.

There's a party at the gravel pits and it's starting already. That turns me off. I hate to smell like booze. I love the smell of pot, but so do other freaks.

"Smell that. Got any?"

Or the narcs: "Look at her. She's been smoking marijuana. Call the police."

Or sympathetic society: "Aw, another victim of society gone astray . . ."

Or, worst of all, Redneck society (sad majority): "I oughta rap you for giving our race such a bad name. If you're gonna inherit the earth, you better shape up or ship out!"

Or the pigs, last and least: "This yours? I'd like to inform you that it is written in the lawbook and derived from the Constitution of the United States that you are in violation of sector two and three chapters one through four, line twenty six . . . forty two and that you are now legally under arrest put your hands against the car spread eagle please Miss and I am required to inform you that this indoctrination of vocal harrassment was compiled by your own juvenile division in preparation for totally deranging your burnt minds with a congregation of useless intellectual terms derived from our leatherbound Funk and Wagnalls and the speed of my intricate work in carefully explaining this to you so that you can understand it fully should be given to the milewise computer corporation speed speech course you have the right to remain silent but don't because we want to get as much from you as possible so this looks good anything you do or say from this point on will be used against you in a court of law because you're on candid camera and you're also being recorded so I guess you must fully understand your rights because you've probably heard them before anyway so, ah, Joe, turn off the tapes for a second good, now Miss stay up against the car arms over your head and please take off your clothes so we can search them and it will save time in the J.C. but don't worry we are specially equipped with blankets so we can't get sued if you get a cold and you really don't have to worry about saying anything, Miss, the tapes are prerecorded anyway . . . anyway . . . anyway . . . anyway . . . (click).

I've decided that my life is controlled by time, chance, and circumstance. That is all. As far as death goes, call it sleeping . . . and pretend you don't notice when you find you've been too long dreaming.

"Queen, I'm scared."

"Why?"

"I don't know."

"I do . . ."

"Why, then?"

"The eye you can't see cries the biggest tear."

I don't know what's happening anymore. I have lost the trail and it's so dark up there . . .

• • •

Simon's a loser and I'm a loser and just screw it all there isn't anything to face life for if it's so long and you hate your own guts.

"Here I am again, Queen."

"How can you make yourself apparent to me?"

"I come when I shouldn't. I say things that I don't understand . . . but it's alright."

"Oh, really?"

"Here I am again. That should tell you something in itself, Queen. But I'm hearing you. Always with you . . . why?"

"Because you're not really so aware of me, that's why. We're on our own. Hey. What's the matter with you?"

"Nothing, nothing . . . I swear it."

"Something's . . . why you little bitch!"

"What?"

"Take your head . . . You're fucking straight! I'm here to stop that. You're not worth a thing without me. You have to stay happy, remember? Up and up. You lied to me. Go, then. Go die and be sad and feel the pain. But you're going to need me soon. I'll make you need me very soon . . ."

• • •

Back again and you'll never guess where I am again and yes, I did buy more and that's 40 more and 3 of the other makes me very broke but a few high nights' richer. You're not a bit like Alice, but if you made just a little less sense, you'd make a perfect Chesire cat. But Chesire cats can disappear and leave their grins behind. Feed your head and/or keep your head . . . When they return, the tails fade in last, right after the whiskers, and if they are sad, they simply fade into their grins upside down. P.S. The eyes of Texas are upon you.

• • •

Tonight when I started walking, it was cold. So I walked again. Not really knowing where I was going . . . not really. I stopped on my corner and I felt that same almighty cold that I was so used to and I felt so alone . . . I began to think back on all the smiles and laughing, the running, the dancing, the dreaming . . . the friends. But I only felt the cruel red stoplights, blinking now at that late hour, and the wind from passing cars and then everything blurred together, but for the first time in a long time it wasn't from dope. But I stopped myself right away because I can't let myself cry. It would have scared me and Queen too much. There would be the real me that I thought was dead, just hinting with what was left of sanity, that I *did* feel. Even that old zipped-out kid might have feelings after all. I know

---

Dear, Dear Nancy
I feel guilty not answering you sooner.
I have written letters but I lost your address
I also haven't been able to write very much
at all. I failed four courses last tri-master and
got a B- in one class, writing. See, I'm very,
very, confused, but everything will be alright
someday, I think. Since my letter to you and
Pat at camp-I have aged so, so much. I feel
like an old lady - or something because - well -
I've just learned so much. Too much, maybe,
I don't know. I'm addicted to speed now -
really addicted, and it took me too long
to admit it to myself and the road out
and off is very, very distant. Right now I
can't even see the end. Very soon I may be
put away. In a hospital. With white walls
and nurses and bars. I think - something -
well - I just can't forget you, Nancy
I don't care what happens or what they do
to me but I won't forget you. I love you
for being so very kind to me when I could
still understand people. That last glorious
summer at Camp.... I did give
Seiche a kiss for you, Nancy. He's getting
old too. But he doesn't really change ever.
The colt doesn't have a name yet, but I
think I may call him "Bring a Torch"
because he's so free and simple and easy
to understand that he, like Seiche, helps
me keep in touch with the real world -
which is slipping past me very, very fast.

because the sound of my own sobbing and the feel of my eyes wet and my hair tangled would scare me. I've spent many nights on the verge, right before sleeping. It only showed me how out of control I was, how tired of being out of touch and lost I was. I can't get near a situation that might force me to face where I'm at because I might see how sick I know this is and give up my fight. I am fighting a war on myself that's ripping me soul from mind. And for some reason I won't . . . I can't . . . give up and accept help. I'm going to do this, whatever it is, on my own. It seems that it will be that way, even if it kills me.

My brother says, "Hi". (You remember, don't you?) and he keeps saying what a neat person you are all the time.
I miss you and Pat and summer more than anything else, right now. I just wish I could talk to you again. Maybe if you sent me your telephone number or something. I don't know. If I don't write a lot, it's not anything against you, understand. But I've got to fight so hard now. It means so much just to be alive, don't you think? Just to be . . .

with love and
all my heart,
Pony

Tell me what my mind is saying,
when it says, "You must be sad;
through all the games you're playing
you must feel pretty bad."
And still if I'm alone,
my mind says, "You're not lonely."   Boom Boom Yeah
I don't quite understand.
No, I don't quite understand.
Tell me what my eyes are seeing
when they see there's no one there.   Boom Boom Yeah
If I'm not alone, I'm agreeing
I can't have much to share.

Why?
strive to be,
when being at all
serves no particular purpose?
I've been meaning to talk to you about
it for some time

Ba Baw Baw Bli Blip
Ba Baw Baw Bli Blip
Ba Baw Baw Baw Baw Baw
Baw Baw Baw strum EEEK strum

"LOVE WILL GET YOU THROUGH TIMES OF NO SEX
better than
SEX WILL GET YOU THROUGH TIMES OF NO LOVE"
ah wrote that on the wall, yes ah did.
deed ah dood it, yes ah dood.

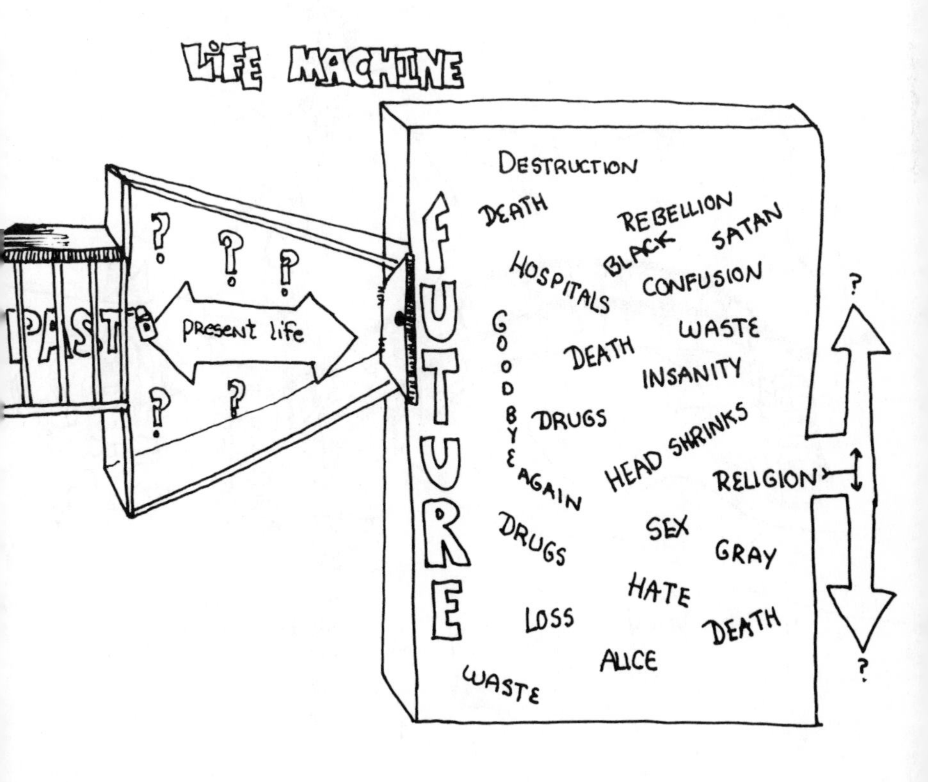
LIFE MACHINE
PAST
present life
FUTURE
DESTRUCTION
DEATH
REBELLION
BLACK
SATAN
HOSPITALS
CONFUSION
GOODBYE AGAIN
DEATH
WASTE
INSANITY
DRUGS
HEAD SHRINKS
RELIGION
DRUGS
SEX
GRAY
HATE
LOSS
DEATH
ALICE
WASTE

Lucy in the Sky with Diamonds

Part two

Lost time, useless time
Long empty useless time

Please understand, I'm only lonely

What time is it?

All I can see is the second hand sweeping.
Climbing, falling, like a constant ferris wheel.
I attach neon to the numbers, red and yellow.
What time is it?
All I can see is the face of the clock.
White, blank, staring with no purpose.
I paint it black like night, purple and blue.
What time is it?
All I can see are the many dark dots.
Spaced for minutes; perfect, yet useless.
I let them be crowds of people, gray and green, gray and green . . .

Lost time, useless time, long, empty, useless time.

Monday, Dec. 2

Wow. This is really a bummer. It's Monday. It's the new trimester. Already here I am. In the library again missing a class or two that I haven't even been to yet. Know something? I'm also tripping again. I've got to keep up. Oh fuck why am I waiting? I don't want to die . . . I just wish all this was over because I guess I really see no use in it anymore. If I pull out now, everyone else will keep going. I have to pull out before I go thoroughly insane. But if I do, I'll get left behind. No one else is going to wait for me. I don't want to be left behind . . . fucking ironic. Yeah, Ha Ha. I get so sad living like I am now . . . I want to get out of school and into something. What, I don't know. An institution. Yeah, and J.C., maybe. And *not* to get back at my parents. I love them. No, I hate them . . . I don't know. But for *me.* Just for once . . . something for me. For *my* head, not theirs. The old shrink? That was for them, really. Sending me there religiously made my burden on them lighter. It made them, well, somehow . . . less responsable. Responsable. I've heard that before. Having good responses? Bullshit. *Not* being responsable for me or my actions.

Family Service? Shit. Who was that for? Hubert? No, eventually mother, father, and brother. Not me. No bullshit for me. Try another. Reachout? Hey now. That place is so fucking screwed . . . that was for Brendan, Jerry, and to pull the wool over parent-dears' eyes to make them think I was turning to good. To keep their chins up and out . . . One Way? Definitely for Detective Reddy and the rest of them to show them that I was going to keep my promise. At least that's how it started. In fact, that's the thing that was the most for me . . . for a while. Then it was for the staff and, like Reachout, for the parents. And for Tom. Christain Life? Well, it wasn't good enough. Then they wanted me to go to Christain Life because Brent Wiser was their friend and told them things. Very sneaky. But again, people can do their own thing, and that's cool. But again, again, no one can force *anyone* to be a Christain if they want a true Christain. No bullshit. I'll stick to One Way. If I stick to anything at all.

Let me figure this out. **Reachout:** sucks, personally. **One**

Way: total confusion . . . no comment. **Family Service:** O.K. for some people. Not too bad. **Shrink:** God knows not *that* one, maybe try again, but I doubt it. **Dean:** Good old Dean. Wonder how he's doing? **Brendan:** Good friend, at his cost. Am very open with him. He's easy to talk to. Gotta trust someone. **Dan:** Beautiful friend. He cares, so far. **Neil:** Mellow/rowdy. Good guy. Don't know him too well. **Fred:** Another good guy. All of those guys are my friends. I really like them. **Dodger:** Well . . . total confusion, no labels, please. **Ray:** Good guy, don't know too well. In trouble. **Margo:** Good chick, pretty. Again, don't know too well. **Tim:** Who the hell knows? **Nic:** ? **Terry:** O.K., I think. **Zombie:** O.K., I think, as far as this school goes. **Teachers, Miss Cambridge:** Understanding. **Study Hall and Hall Monitors . . .** "Vanila Piles" and "Saucy": O.K. (keep 'em on your side). **Sadie:** Want to help her. She needs someone. Fights, but not long grudges. **Cherries:** Definitely mellow. Understanding. Also needs someone, but on the right track. **Siren:** Rowdy, needs guiding, but really good chick. **S'lins:** I only wish I knew. **Simon:** Oh God, he needs someone very badly to guide him. I feel like his mother and he says *I* make *him* feel old. What *does* he really want? **Tom:** Where are you? **Mother:** Stay loose, I'll take care of myself. **Father:** Stay loose (get loose first). I'll grow up someday for you. **Spring Valley Police:** Sorry, and thanks anyway. **City of Spring Valley:** What the hell are you growing to? Where did you go? **Brett Greene:** Needs help but God knows I can't give it to her but through One Way. **Luke:** Extremely mellow. Good guy to talk to. **Cris:** Help, etc. **Reddy:** Wish I could prove to him that I'm not all that bad. I don't lie that much anymore, and I'm sorry. **Seiche:** I love more than anything I have ever felt for. He listens, and he talks, silently. The best way. I could cry when I realize what patience he has. **Colt:** Mellow/rowdy, don't know yet. **Spatts:** Sorry. "The horse with the tear in his eye." **Barkley (Brie)** (my sheepdog): Patience. Loves me more than I ever took notice of. **Sunny** (Tom's Sheltie): Understanding. Sweet. **H.Ball**(kitten): Mellow. **Edie** (his mother): Feminine. **Rats:** Patient. **Solomon** (tortoise): Very, very lonely. Cut.

This is totally ridiculous. (Got carried away.)

Well, Pony! Hi! I haven't seen you for a while.— Hi. — How ya been? — O.K., I guess. — Oh. How's Seiche? — Fine (stay away from him). — Can we go riding some time? — Yeah, sure (not on Seiche). — Bye, gotta go. — We all do. — What? — Nothing. Bye. — Bye.

SILENCE. How are you? — Existing. — How's that? — Not living at least. — How do you think you feel right now? — O.K. (bullshit, tell him you're sad). — That's good to hear. — (Oh, well it was O.K. to tell him that. Now at least he feels good.)

• • •

I'm confused. — I've been there, too. — I want to die. — So did I. — I'm going to kill myself. — We'll miss you. — Yeah, I bet. You and who else? — Me and Jesus Christ.

• • •

Who ever taught you to see? (huh?) — Huh? — Did someone tell you exactly how? — No. What do you mean? — Do you ever want people? (I do, say you do . . .) Huh? (I don't want to be this way but I find it . . . hard to tell you who I am and how I feel, please understand I'm only lonely, not crazy, yet). Please understand . . . ((She is crazy.))

• • •

Seiche: I love you. I'm coming to the barn soon. Your home. Mine, too? Look at all the people. When there are that many, they become merely "people." No labels — I love them all. Half of them I silently greet and they don't know me and I don't know them really, I just pretend I do. Makes me feel more together — Help — I'm flying — come down, come down, that's it. Mellow out. O.K. Now — let's try again. For the third time? And I ask myself, is it really worth it? Really? No, I say twice. Yes, I say once. HELP — I say three times.

OPINION OF SCHOOL: Sucksalmightyshitcrick, and I thoroughly love it. I just wish someone would wait for me. I sometimes see where I am, you know. BEHIND. Hating it, loving writing here, but getting behind. Hating my guts.

ALL THE TIME.

Between a warning and a deep, deep sorrow

Tuesday, Dec. 3

Last night I cruised with Dan and I warned him that I was totally bummed out and that he would end up that way, too, after talking to me. He told me that if he wasn't so uptight he'd hug me. I don't know. Saw Tom's friend in Bay Mall who read some scripture. Then, the Artful Dodger appeared, Shelly and then Simon. I'm scared of him. I felt too much like nothing, so I pulled out Gillette's best and cut my arm a little. I hadn't done that in a long time, but it felt good. It gives me something to think about. At the laundry entrance, I took some street salt from the pavement and held it against the cuts. Now that felt bad. Or as Artful would say, "IT HURT SO GOOD." My eyes started watering and my hand went numb and I stood in there, laughing, watching the salt crystals dissolve and bubble into the open cuts and mix into my blood. Then I felt like crying, or maybe dying, I don't know. Dan grabbed me from a couple of oncoming cars that I was not going to let hit me anyway. Dan and Fred and Artful are the kind of friends that are hard to come by. Burnt or ex-burnt, extremely crude when it's appropriate, sympathetic when it's appropriate, or crazier than all hell when it's not so appropriate. But that's cool.

That ivory dove on my choker is sliding around and it sounds like when Sadie tried to take the collar off of her dead dog, Lucky . . . Whew — that one passed over. For a second I thought I was going to get mean and nasty because I got a cold wave again. Definition of cold wave — sudden and unexplainable depression that can induce suicide or an extreme feeling of uselessness . . . I feel another one coming on . . . think — quick — happy things . . . I love Seiche — he's so beautiful . . . the sun on the snow . . . in the trees . . . God . . . birds . . . people . . . time . . . ridiculousness . . . insanity satisfaction . . . wind, rain, snow, sun, sleet, the sky, space, the sea . . . life itself, sometimes . . . clocks, damn 'em all . . . Artful . . . Dan . . . Fred . . . eternal high . . . sometimes . . . somewhere . . . dreamers. . . past . . . poems . . . somehow . . . these aren't helping much so screw 'em.

People are really walking close to me today. They come straight twards me, then turn and go somewhere . . . I sometimes believe they're aiming guns or knives at me . . . or talking to me . . . like the bookshelves. The bigger the library, the more voices. The librarian just walked by and saw my scars. Big Felix. I've decided that if I die, I want to die either in the field, the bowling alley, but mainly in the library. Strange. Not too many people die in libraries. I could spend my life here. It's so beautiful. Like a phonebooth with burnt-out lights. People leave you alone and that's why it's so beautiful. Slow down, you move too fast . . . I ain't so sure anymore. Rude, crude and socially ultra-sonic. Like peanut butter and gunpuppy. Peanut butter makes you horny. It's a proven fact. R.O.A. Syndicate—all beds reserved. etc. Copyright, patent pending.

There is a life here, I feel,
Somewhere in between
The bloody Satan's Star
And the wrist of bracelet scars
I don't know what it means

December 3, (night:11:45)

Chase is dead. Dan is freaked. I'm dead, in a way. Not physically. I love things. I love Dan. Very, very much . . . Does anyone understand? For tomorrow . . . I must be there as I should be.

Dec. 4

I think I should be dead because I feel like I am but I'm not I'm still here and other people can see me but I know one thing only that I'm not going to change tomorrow or a week from tomorrow and in that sense I can only get worse and I won't be able to take it and I can't communicate to anyone about how I feel I can't make them understand without joking around a little because I cried wolf once and now I have to pay the price. The godamned eternal price. I guess I shouldn't be afraid to die now. It can't hurt as bad as I'm hurting today.

Hey, it's alright. (Not really.) Marsha the rat died last night, or this morning. All I can see is that convulsing, constricting gut and her heaving and sinking into a coma and fighting for air. It was cruel to let her die that way. I wanted her to die of old age (and she did) but I didn't want her to suffer so much. I know she did that. Half vegetable-minded rodent . . . milk and honey colored . . . seething with viruses and insanity, I said everyday that I'd have her put to sleep the next day. Last night I touched her and she hunched to attack. I was tempted to slam her on a table, but I don't think I could have done it. So she lived, and died. Just like me. I will too. She lived through a lot. The day after I bought her, Tom ran for the third time. Joella and Grandad died in January, Spatts broke his foot. Then it was my turn. [Breaking bones and spraining things.]

Chase is dead now. Strange. I felt like crying . . . He never said anything mean to me. I overheard . . . well, shit. I was looking for a quote to remember, and I heard Mom talking to Tom about it.

"I really loved that kid," she said.

Tom mumbled something.

"Well you know," she said, "he took you in off the streets when no one else would."

I was at the landing of the stairs and what I saw and heard sent me into a silent kind of shock. I just caught Tom with his hand on the doorknob of his room, that now reads Sunblast Studios on the door. The scenes flashed like a multi-media slide-show in my skull of the past — Tom's hand on the same doorknob a year ago, two years ago, three . . . as his room and he changed. First music and rings on his fingers, then I don't remember . . . taking apart flashlights to make pipes, then the hard drugs and the blacklight posters, HUGE black light, bed on the floor, then those damned incense-holding Buddahs with the flames . . . and then the tie-dyed sheet on the wall, and then . . . the Satanic altar against the wall . . . With me standing so small at his door, waiting for him to sleep so I could put out the candles that flickered so dangerously under the Satanic star. The goathead. I didn't understand it but it scared me. Chase was in on it when Tom first came to this school three years ago, with his hair down to his back, one gold earring, a black leather jacket, a huge medallion eye reading, "stone free" . . . and a pistol in his pocket. He'd held that pistol at me before, I just stood, ready . . . The squirrel skin from that week of the trapping "massacre" is still around. The sheet Chase tie-dyed was used temporarily for a sheet on Seiche (it's now ripped up under the mud and snow). Just a few things of his remain anymore. Then I would have been happy to see him go. Now I wish they'd come back . . . I see Tom stand so small and old at my door, waiting to extinguish the candles at my altar, that flicker so dangerously by the wall . . . frequently changing the room for my good (maybe he does love me), ripping down a sign that read "Resume Speed" and other similar things . . . And there we stood, Mom in the hall in her bathrobe, too looking old, me at the landing silently burning with a tear that may never be shed anymore, burning with repulsion and rebellion and an extreme desire to run to him and hold him and tell him everything would be alright. Then Tom, himself, locked in a moment of some dream that had passed long ago, contemplating . . . his eyes were glistening with similar unshed tears from his past . . . "It hurts," he said, and the words hit me hard. Then he turned the doorknob and disappeared. And not once had his gaze caught mine. Not once. But there was something there between us never-the-less. Something between a warning, and a deep, deep sorrow.

Know something, Kevin? I wish I could understand you and your God. You expect a burnt person that is unaware of being physically alive at all, or a person that wants to die because she can't live the two lives at the present, to decide which way to live? If I want to be your hero, I'll narc for you and live with it the rest of my life, which, in this case, will not be very long. If I want to be my own hero, with my people, I'll die for them, too. Or I'll just take the only other alternative, insanity. That, at the present, is too near to ignore and because of this I have to decide now before it's too late to decide.

Thank you much, Kevin. Try blackmail, and while you're at it, take off that dove of yours and put it high on a shelf, closer to where it really belongs. You've got me so screwed up that I don't know whether to go or if I should wait any longer to shun you all now and rest for awhile until the day that you keep scaring me with comes about. Hey, Kevin? Got any fans lying around? It's hot down here. HaHa.

Goodmorning. Not really. I'm dead. So therefore, I'm dead. Truly, on the other hand, I'm dead. But, of course, by the same token, I'm dead.

The garbage man came today and I watched as he piled the garbage into his fat-assed truck. Marsha [my dead rat] was in there, too, and he pulled the lever and squished her along with the o.j. cans. Dan, I love you. No, of course not. I can imagine at least. That I'm sailing . . . no, in a supervised study area, in a hospital for the mentally insane, in a quiet ward. Screw people because they're really weird but of course I don't love them no of course not because it's my fault that I labeled them because I guess I have no right. I haven't seen the Lord's prayer for a hell of a long time.

Dan is going home tonight. I love him. I can't help feeling scared . . . it hurts, and I'm so scared . . . and love helps but it hurts, too . . . And I also can't help but think that the last page of this diary must be coming up soon. It burns my eyes but I won't cry. I can't.

Friday, Dec. 6

Dan finally came last night and we danced on the town. He watched as I mutilated my arm with razor blades on the nun's hill. It felt so good to be hurting again.

Monday, Dec.9

Acid-solid-acid trips all weekend . . . don't come down-never no don't come down at all not ever-no . . . Friday when Dan and I got home, the colt's eyelid was dangling by a thread and the whole eye was bared open. Doc sewed it back on and I keeled over in a dead faint. Oh beautiful. My frickin' pen is leaking black ink all over me. Acid Friday night until midnight. I stumbled out to the barn and fell down on the cement in convulsions. Seiche stared at my face and he looked really sad. His eyes cried out but he had a grin on his face and he looked like a little boy that had just broken his first glider. He was big. I took a sycle to him and I wanted him dead, and I'm not sure if it was because he was in so much pain or because I didn't want to have him see me that way. I was ashamed to betray him. He was too real to be there . . . don't you see? He didn't belong. Then my brain had convulsions and I saw him fall in the stall as the sycle blade caught him in the neck. His eyes rolled and he cried out, but not from the pain. He cried out of the hurt of me hitting him. He went town on his knees and his head twisted backwards. His sides stopped heaving and I ran. But I was already at the house. I was in the basement again and Dan was shaking me.

The ceiling turned a kind of puke green and aspirin orange with little stars and when he finally left I was alone again and I laughed into the mirror and it melted. I woke out of it in the morning and took a shower. Trella walked in. We walked around for awhile. Dan's at night. Stoned again. Super freaked, I guess, watching "My Fair Lady" on the TV. Guess what? He told me he loved me. Acid or what's left of brains? I don't know anymore . . . I don't understand . . . and some frickin' tripper that's never really straight enough to know keeps telling me I don't even care . . .

To the Blue

They try so very hard to type my mind and
kind from the insides of my pockets and a manilla file
with my past crimes . . . my pocket's past.
But 3M doesn't know who I am, neither does the computer . . .
They don't know who I am.
Their files can never file me, they have nothing . . . nothing
but yesterday's coat and old pockets. Right or illegal, wrong or clean . . .
Yes, clean. Ha ha ha, you blew it again. You can't hold me.
Your charges won't change me. Even though some pieces of my mind aren't
quite as special as they were . . . before you . . . it's going to be a day.
You never knew me . . . you won't ever.
You don't know who I am.

Scared to end it; afraid to go on

Mon. (continued)

It's a Monday afternoon already. Screw life. Screw Mondays. I guess I'll have to decide now what I'm going to do. Humans usually like things easy and I'm no exception. I'll drop school and follow my head. Find a job maybe, drown. Maybe if I got busted and asked them, then maybe ... well shit, it's just a wierd enough idea to work. I do have ideas, considering my mind schemes a hell of a lot. But anyway, I think I'd like to feel a little more about now. Maybe I should climb a tree on a rainy afternoon. That helps you feel a little bit. Clears up the clouds with a wipe of the fingers. Like stirring soup with barley, it's got to settle sometime, you know.

Well, it's 12:50. How do I feel? . . . Huh. That's odd. But not really, I guess. Here I am again in the situation of not being able to hack questions like that at all. I can't define what I feel or why I can't feel or maybe I just don't realize that I'm feeling at all. It's not there. Or something.

The colt is very, very beautiful. So is Seiche. How I feel for them. Just like the night . . . Don't cry . . . when I think of the night. The night . . . the night . . . The cold, the silence, the solitude, the multitude of life in forms, I guess . . . for just being alone and still and different from them. Shhh . . . it's alright. It'll be alright. Like an accident. Half-and-almost-dead people are hugged and cradled and lied to. I wish I were in a dark corner or something with something to hug like a stuffed animal.

It'sss . . . See that? Scared the all hell out of me. Some friend pulled the fuckin' fire alarm. Went outside, came back in, and he pulled it again. Beautiful. Had to grab my jacket so they wouldn't search it. Can't draw either. My hand's not that coordinated. Wow. Damn life. Too scared to end it and afraid to go on. Just back inside. I just want to brush up on the last lines.

While chasing my traces for years and days,
The car with the gun and the bars finds its way . . .
Behind me, behind me, are people to see . . .
And you can just bet that they're waiting for me.
Then three vinyl horses I called for from space
Came burning and kicking, and hindered the chase.
Above me, above me, and yes, I believe . . .
They tell me to stay, but I'm going to leave.
While rounding the corner and topping the hill
He follows the arrows and all becomes still.
Beside me — I run, for there's no time to stay,
The white rabbit's waiting, I cannot delay.
Run children, run for me, step in my road.
But bring along loving, it's awfully cold.
Behind you, above you, beside you, and then,
You follow the rabbit and do it again.
As the sky darkens deep for a mellowing tune,
The sun collides fiercely and singes the moon.
The fool on the hill stands up from his chair,
I know that he is: but he thinks he's not there.
Behind from the mountain of silky thread grass,
Rises a sunlamp of fiery orange glass.
Around me, clouds gather, and still I go on,
So little to do yet so much to get done.
A castle is burning and I was once there.
I think that I'll miss it; I know I don't dare.
I lost the warm love that I'd brought for a cloak,
And being pursued I can't see through the smoke.
Run children, run with me. Walk in my trail . . .
But bring along loving, you're bound for a sail.
Behind you, above you, beside you and then . . .
You follow the arrows, and try it again.
Looking aside, though the light's getting dim . . .
The Cheshire cat's smile is increasingly grim.
A woven noose tied to the tip of his perch . . .
I followed my footsteps, and ended the search.
Behind, silvered stallions will snort in alarm,
The cat shift his gaze to the rope by his arm.
Above, I believe, they can no longer see . . .
You can only suggest — that they're waiting for me.
Run children, run from me . . . stop where you stand.
The time to escape will be soon right at hand.
Behind you, above you, beside you, and then . . .
You count all the gravestones and pass me again.

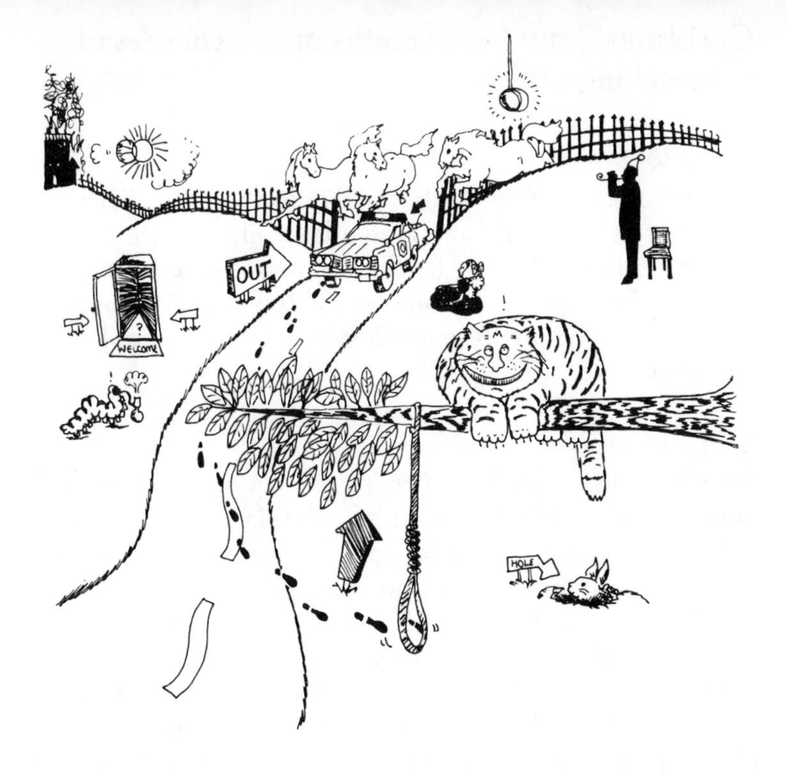

Dec. 11

Don't ever make a mistake. I keep all my special things in a dark box because if I carry them, the pigs will confiscate them and handle them and investigate them and give them back only sometimes, and then in a plastic police official evidence bag — then they lose their specialness somehow.

Weekend of Friday the 13th

Tell 'em it'll shine when it shines . . .
Dan came over and helped me shovel horse stalls.

Dec. 21

How odd. Yesterday Dan and I and Cris, Pastor Lavin, and Ed DeForest met at the coffeehouse. Dan freaked out. He hung up on me tonight. No, I hung up on him. Can't remember. He's going away. The preacher told him that I was "of the Devil" and he rebuked me. Yes, it was me. I *had* to hang up.

Christmas. I put two wreaths on the cherries of the local pig car.

Dec. 26

I believe I am useless. Only for dying, that's all. I'm very, very, very tired of life and I am a loser like Simon. No one can really help even if I let them. The sad overpowers the laughter. Sorry, child. It's all over. Throw it in now, because you won't know life from death if they lock you up. It is all very much over. I want to sleep.

Sun., Dec. 28

After finding a bunch of Tom's fuck-you-it's-all-your-fault notes left around the house for me to see last night and going to bed with wet eyes, I woke up (and I know, like you, that sleep's the only possible hope of escape from my mind that I have without harming myself, right?) with Mom telling me there was help needed in putting up a mailbox. I got up. There was a big confrontation about school absences. I ran out to the barn to be with Seiche. Never even have any hope of me telling them. Flat out. "I have reason to believe, a reason that is too difficult to word, that I am slipping mentally, in other words going crazy, and that just because you tell me I'm not alone, that makes it no better at all. I have the same reason to believe that this illness, as I will call it, should be treated promptly before it gets out of hand, out of mind, out of hope. Thankyou. Stomp, stomp, stomp, stomp, SLAM!"

Mon. Dec. 29 (Dad's birthday. Written in the living room, before going for a walk.)
I understand it's been awhile. Well, of course it has. I have not been here so long, that's all. I've been stumbling a bit. Certainly if you had been there — although you had no obligation and it's probably better that way anyway — you would have seen it too. Just that way, it's been. Been awhile, yes it has. All I need is what I had and what I see ahead. What I do actually see should not be asserted as an improbability. It is after Christmas. Yes, it is. It's the twenty-ninth now. It is my father's date of birth. Get ready. People get yourselves ready. I had a sudden-but-common-felt urge to go to the street tonight. Tonight soon. To the snow . . . to the night . . . to the indefinite stretch of asphalt that supports these dark places I frequently visit; frequently hide in. I think I will. Yes, I think I'll go. To my jungle. The closest I can find, because a forest is not half the lonliness of a city. Just a street. There are these dark places, and I do go there and I can't quite order this all in my brain. Accidents do happen; people die. Put it together. Get ready. Very, very. Yes, it has — been awhile, I understand.

When I am with myself, I am alone.

Dec. 31

I'll tell ya. This is really just it, that's all. The last fucking day of this fucking year and I am *all* alone. Me and my acid. I'm too burnt to compose a mural of the year's happenings like I did last year. Besides, I couldn't cut anything from a magazine that could explain it. My head can't, I know. Didn't sleep at all last night. I sat there in bed; here in bed, laughing and spraying breath spray all over my mouth. Tastes like sterilized cardboard this morning. But what is it worth? Without anyone, it's amazing what lonely people will do. Lonely like me. That's right. Like me. Dan has gone to South America. He left on the twenty-second. I'm going out alone again. To walk and hope I don't trip on an occasional highway. P.S. Got a friend in a dark, dark room.

I'm not into trying to figure anything out today. Twenty just doesn't do it anymore. It took twenty-three yesterday and I barely buzzed. Sorry, Donlan, You're not together enough to write. Go get high. Then come back. If you can.

Ashes don't even burn

January 1

Another historical one. Should I start with last year's heading? "Happy New year. Nothing's changed." But I can't say that anymore, can I? Because things *are* different. For worse, most of the way. I got the colt. That was good. He may be a good showhorse someday. I named him "Cinnabar Foxe." Eighth grade was the year I grew up. I met Brendan the cop, and in ninth grade he left somehow. I met Roy and Kevin, also cops. They were nicer to me than anyone my own age. I stopped going to the bowling alley, and started school in the Willowood Senior High. Sadie's horse, Spatts, broke his leg. Sadie got a puppy. The first person I met at school I met in the can, smoking during lunch. She introduced me to Stash, and I started going out with Rico. I found Simon again. But for the most part of the year, it's been Dan. Started heavy zip and acid. How can it be another year? I haven't figured out the last one yet. See? I told you things move on whether you stay or truck, live or not. You can either ride with it or drop back. I have some catching up to do. Like everything, I'm behind in life, too. But it doesn't matter. I'm on the verge of seeing a shrink again, going to a mental hospital, and the only reason I haven't been suspended from school yet is because I registered late, and the computer doesn't know who I am. I'm on the verge of a self-inflicted death.

Today I slept until 3:00! I also dreamed that I lived in a white house that was lifted from its site during the winter and dropped — in the spring — in a muddy brook. Seiche and a gray horse lived in the local saddle shop, and when I got to summer camp I decided I didn't like it. We returned home and I purchased a china angel — with a green robe, a chain around the neck like a butterfly, and inflated arms — at a flea market.

Following that, Barkley jumped on me and woke me up. I trained the colt, fed the horses, forgetting again, to clean their stalls. Technically, the colt is a yearling today, but not really until April. Monday night I did a fourth of blotter acid and really got bammed. There was an orchestra and angels singing and hanging in the windows of the Children's Store. I found Terry and Stash. Only a little gut rot this time. I stayed at Big Mike's until late. Went to bed, but couldn't even close my eyes. Last night I did a whole hit of acid and nothing happened. I met Kevin. He got kicked in the jaw and it's all swollen but he still manages to smile, even though it looks like it hurts. He still wants names . . . He actually thinks I'd give them to him. He's nuts . . .

Sadie broke or sprained her ankle so I'm stuck with the horses. I think I'm tired, but I don't know why. "Still, tomorrow's gonna be another workin' day, and I'm tryin' to get some rest. That's all, I'm tryin', to get some rest." [Paul Simon's *An American Tune] Amen.*

P.S. Happy New Year. I think.

• • •

Fuck you, nothing personal or anything, just that you're here. Or there. Or wherever. Or something. That's all. I can't accept you even for what you are. I can ignore you, but I can't agree with you. I can only leave you as you are. I have no desire to change you. I have not the power, nor the time. You won't accept me for what I believe, so I must also assume that you will ignore me, leave me alone. When I say this, it's not because I hate who you are, I hate only your presence. Anyone's presence. Just being here . . . or wherever you really are, makes you my enemy. You can love me. You can say you love me. But I can't return anyone's love. No one's. In defense of your feelings for me; you may use that excuse for this: you will not believe what I feel is true because I'm constantly speaking and saying nothing at all. I have not the ability to say what I really feel. I have not the right to believe that what I think I feel is what

I do feel. I do not know you. I never have known anyone. So I am leaving. Either way, as lost as I am with you, I have no way of loving you, even though I might have at one time. I do think I love you, but . . . that's not all that matters anymore. What I think has no significance to my actual feelings; what they are I don't know. You see (or you might now), I am not who I am. The person that you think I am, the me you know, is not me at all. Not even a part of me. I am lost to myself, and to others, like you. That's right, Dan, I'm lost to you. I have heard too much and used opinions of other people to go on. I have reached the point where I can no longer tolerate my thoughts. My thoughts never cease. They are dangerous. I feel that I'm hurting. Like there is strycnine in my brain. Eating it away. Burning it to ashes and smoke and dust. Whipping it apart. Until every bit is gone. Or permanently lame. You can't build a thing out of ashes. Not one thing. Ashes are only dead and sterile. And nothing ever comes of them once they get the way they are. I do not hate you. I am afraid of getting more people anywhere near me, that is all. You are here, so are others; and others are gone, too. You can not get here from there; I can not get here at all. There is no way to make what is lost now come back. Dan, understand please . . . Ashes don't even burn.

Jan. 5

Sunday . . . Well, it's back-to-school brain-savings time again. Merry Christmas, Happy New Year . . . Do you have a pass? Got any zip? I'm bringing nine pigeons home tomorrow. And then I'm going to that shrink whose name sounds like a blacksmith's. My brainsmith and mind farrier. Then this interior decorator is coming to try to change this pit [my bedroom]. I guess only I know that all I will be bringing to school tomorrow is my notebook and some paper, and maybe a calendar so I can tell people what day it is all day. I might like to know someday why it is such a crime to be lonely. Principal's out for me. So are the teachers. There's nothing I can say. See, the problem with living is that you get older and you get behind for your age and you eventually forget everything. The problem with taking a year or two off is you get behind. The problem with dying is that, even though you don't get any more behind (unless you're not a Christain, from what I've heard) you can't come back.

Maybe that's O.K. by me. I'm not really sure yet. Or maybe it should be "anymore." Am I:

Anti-Christ ____________ Satanist ____________
Witch ____________ Christain ____________
Troubled ____________ Insane ____________
Chemically dependent ____________
Horse lover ____________ Rowdy ____________
Bitch ____________ Criminal ____________
Pig-hater ____________ Intelligent ____________
Burnt out ____________ Lover ____________.

HELP. All I want to know is what I am and no one can tell me who I am, but only I can listen and try to put it all together and maybe someday it'll all be alright.

I haven't really found a person who will listen and not expel me . . . or bust me . . . or inform on me . . . or tell me I'm wrong. Tell me — like you — that I'm a wrong person. Tell me that, and there will be nothing more to say. I've had it. I've had you. And still, there is nothing.

Monday, Jan. 6th

Well, here I am in school again, more or less. I'm satisfied just being here and having an empty mind. I guess I'm not really feeling alright. It's the comparison between the past and the present that will someday kill me. I have changed, yes. I've learned how to treat people in certain situations, my hair is darker, I am no longer an outsider with boys, I am fairly burnt out, I have another armful of scars on my arm from the coven, and generally, I am much more screwed up than I have ever been before.

It hassles me to think that I wasted all that time when I first met Brendan trying to pull it over on him that I was a junkie. Really, I can't blame him one bit for casually ignoring me. He knows. Sure, he knows. The things I saw, the flashbacks, were just my head going screwy. The pills I did take were either unidentified or fairly harmless. I can never be sure about the combinations, however. I sometimes sit in school and wonder if Brendan would even care if he knew what was happening to me. "If only's" aren't worth anything but imagination, but I guess I wish I could buy back the days when we were in a comfortable talking situation. My silence in these was trying to convey a message. And he got it. Help. Then he asked me something I couldn't answer. "What can I do to help?"

I didn't see just how fucking lonely I was. Face it, Spring Valley is a prison for all of us. At least the new squad doesn't have a screen. That's a break. But I suppose they still treat you like street dogs if you get busted, even if you aren't behind a "Kennel-aire." Using a fairly understandable excuse that if you act like a street dog, you get busted like a street dog. And so on and so forth.

Well, now I have two frozen feet that refuse to produce any movement. I have been to Willowood and I left at 11:00. Walked the main drag after hitching a ride from Green Street. Returned to the Country Kitchen after spotting cherries; I was almost sure it was a highway pig until I saw the baby blue siren. It was Roy. He had to go. I stayed out until now, which is late.

January 7

The easiest way for me to continue life would be to live apart from my family. Way apart. I don't hate them, but they make it more confusing with their questions. If they ignore me, that doesn't help either. I still love them, but they don't — and there's no way they can — help. Give me an apartment downtown or even in another city or state. With a job to support me, I *could* be alright. Someday, maybe.

Dear Dan, Now it's Tuesday and I was hoping to see you sooner, but I just found out you wouldn't be home until Saturday. A lot has happened since you left, babe. Too much. But I still love you. You are a beautiful, caring, gentle person to me. I need you so *very* much right now. Where is your God now? He's either there or He's not. Same with Lucifer, right?

Dan, I'm going to admit something to you. I am different. So what else can be new? I am sure it doesn't sound different, me being different. Too many things have changed. Oh, God, Dan I love you . . . I can't think anything else. I need your hand here to hold. I might even need your silence. Just be here. I miss you. My heart hurts . . . Another 30. Oh damn it. I pray that you come back while I'm still here. Just like with Joella . . . machines kept her alive for days. Speed keeps me alive . . .

"Here lies Joan Donlan, her death has gotten her through time of no hope." And scrawled at the bottom, "but Satan killed her and we all know that."

January the eighth, Wednesday

Dead or terminal people think back [at the past]. I am. Mainly I cry for unfinished people. Endings that could have been happy . . . maybe. Wow. See, there's nothing to save tomorrow. I'm already dead. Dan, I'm sorry this was timed so badly. Do you understand? No, of course not. Just don't try to understand. It's so hard to pray, but I do. I try. I had plans of waiting, but I can wait no longer. I can only pray now that He will take me with him. Wow, just think. It's finally over. Have I found the truth? I don't understand. I don't try to understand. Squad 217 just said [over the police radio] what I'm saying but can only hope will come true. "Be there shortly."

Goodbye, sad word; meaning—
sorrow in leaving; in loss

J. Donlan, Jan. 8, . . . 11:44 p.m.

Saturday, January 11

I am such a hopeless loser I can't even die when I want to. Dan is home. Friday snowed a blizzard, and it's amazingly white outside. It's also below zero. I became a "Christain" whatever that is, and gave Kevin my zip. He told me to pray and I wouldn't even have withdrawl. Bullshit. I'm damn sick, and he can't put one over on me about what it's from . . . I saw Brendan Thursday. We must have had ESP because he talked like he knew and I knew that something had left our friendly relationship. Like he knew all the time. He still cares. What a friend!

Sunday, Jan. 12

Went out on Seiche. Dan came home and gave me a ring and a crop and a Ghana flag. I don't have a thing for him. Only love; *that,* pending. School again tomorrow. Again, again, again.

Monday, Jan 13

Cris called at 7:00 this morning. That was a beautiful move. I couldn't sleep very well last night; the ceiling had something on it. White and shaped like a person, and moving. It scared me. Maybe it didn't . . . so far today I haven't seen Dan. That can be good or bad. I can't be sure. What's-his-name called last night, looking for some LSD. Didn't have any. That ticks me to all hell, too. I was gullable enough to be had like that and give the pig my dope.

Dan and I to Christain Life club for some damn reason. Totally humiliated and fed Weaver (Dan) choc. pudding. Head to head, backs to the floor, overhand from the middle . . . Some night I'll tell you, boy. I WANT SOME ZIP BADLY!!

purple
MICRO DOT.
~~SUCKS~~

change of MIND.

Tuesday, January the 14th

Ain't nothin much to write about. I have no zip, Kevin has it. I have no acid, Kevin has it. He may not even have it anymore, and either way, he won't give it back. No one will sell me any, and I only have two bucks anyway. All together my desire for life is at an all time low and nothing available really appeals to me at all. I have no religion, as far as I know. I have no care for living in times like this. Depressions. No money, no dope, no enthusiasm. It really makes these long days hard to take.

I'm very tired of long hallways. Really very tired. Damn all these fuckers that keep walking by me. Fuck them. They want to see what I'm writing about them.

Wednesday, January 15th

No. That's bullshit. I cashed a check on my way to school, slept too late after hearing K2 [on the police radio]. Got some money again, and here's my schedule. 1. Count money. 2.(?) Look for a pusher here. 3.(?) Wait until tonight 4.(?) Call about tonight 5.(?) Find Kevin and ask him. 6.(?) Find Kevin and jump him. 7.(?) Find Kevin and kill him. 8.(?) Sit here like an ass all day.

P.S. Dear Tom,

Please don't play detective for Mom. I never went looking for proofs that you were screwed up, because I needed no proof. I know that if you need proof, then maybe I can do alright *on my own.* In other words, if it doesn't show, *leave it be. It will work out.*

The day wears on . . .

Mother asked me very coolly if I was chemically dependant. She said Tom's the narc. Fucking paranoid. ZAP! Oh well, just saving them grief, considering that they can't help me unless I decide to help myself . . . in *any* situation, I told them I wasn't.

Well, it's another afternoon. I'm getting very experienced in selling dope. My thirteen bucks bought me sixty-five hits of Dexedrine, and someone else's five bucks bought them twenty-five, which I gave to Smilee. Only he sold them four for a dollar, instead of five for a dollar, the way I bought them. I love it. It uplifts my self-image and spirit. Crushes my depression away. Then turns it around and slaps me in the face. Beautiful.

I have a feeling Dan and I are failing somehow. There's just something . . . there . . . I'm lonely for a good ear like Brendan or Roy . . .

Tomorrow I have to take some tests to see how competent I am. See, I could have been much more negative. Like: "to see *if* I'm competent." Don't think I don't wonder sometimes, but oh well, "I wantz to bveee allone." So I'll just leave it that way. I should be sleeping. My head just won't quit. Not only that, my eyes won't shut. Makes it difficult (sigh). I'll force myself. ZZZZZZZZZZZZZZZZZZZZZZZZZZZZZ

P.S. Goodnight Roy.

P.S.S. Zorrite!

January 16th

Bought 6 mikes [micro-dot] today. Took some ink blot tests, and two others. Artful Dodger goes into St. Vincent's tomorrow at 6:00. I think Kevin narced on me. I could tell, not only because Mother told me, but in that everything she said was in his words. Oh, dear lady, what you don't know.

Oh dear people in the world what you don't know!! Ha!
Its blessing or food.
Too much [illegible]. I can't
remember and I don't understand
[illegible] but it is alright
[illegible] tight! [illegible] Ha!
[illegible]
[illegible]

PARENTS: SEE HOW MUCH FAITH YOUR DAUGHTER HAS IN YOU? IF YOU'RE READING THIS, DOES SHE REALLY HAVE A REASON TO?

January 17

I can tell it's going to be another useless, ridiculously empty, blowout-brained weekend. Missed Led Zeppelin concert (that's tonight), but Tom told me they'd been sold out anyway. Oh well. I think I miss Artful already. He's gone to drug treatment. Sold himself out, too.

January 18

Oh, well, I guess I'm in the mood for sitting in a room and really talking to someone. But that can't be, not tonight. I feel like talking about myself, and about games people play. I almost feel it's urgent because I just realized that I've been talking to all these "weekend" people, like parents, and I've been playing games around them. Going around myself, doing a neat little skirt around my mind and my feelings, and generally where I'm at. I think it's time I layed myself out on a table (not literally) and picked my brains apart peice by peice. In other words try to "realize" myself a little. I'm afraid I haven't listened to myself, my *real* self for a long time. Either because I've been too burnt, or just too surface.

So many people have asked me who I'm trying to hurt. Well, if it's my parents, it's damn unconcious. If that's possible at all, because obviously I'm hurting them, but I feel guilty as hell about it all.

There will always be something to get over

I'm back. Sadie told me some awful news. Apparently, a cop called her mother and told her that the cops were keeping tabs on me and watching what I do. Oh marvelous, here we go again, one, two, three — and all that.

Sometimes I wonder when my head will really be down. My body, my mind, my blood, my skin, it all contains acid and acid all is eating at my system. I feel it even when I'm crashed. I just realized I haven't been crashed out for a hell of a long time. Wow, at least a week, maybe two.

Bring back the roses, the cold flapping canvas . . . the crowds of ridiculously game-masked, grief-eaten people who stared dumbly, even horrified, at the gold casket with the brass handles, with roses leaning up to it and a wreath of roses encircling the lid of the thing, all running the same thoughts through their brains, realizing there was a body and nothing more where three days ago a person had been. Maybe it was some personal anticipation, inside themselves, being hit hard with something so cold—so real—and none of them really knowing how to act . . . there she rested with her white cushions and gold cross and yellow dress; clayish, neatly folded hands. Placed by some morbid artist, or maybe a deathbed doctor, the same one that brushed her eyes closed, for the last time.

Bring back the years she lived, the years she's lost. That can't be. It won't be. It's not going to happen. Bring back the roses, yes, and the morbid memories of only death, nothing of her life. Bring out photos, only a few—but well searched out for some hidden message in the black and white of her face. Some anticipation; questioning eyes . . . Deep into something that can't be anymore. Something that doesn't matter even if there was an answer in her eyes. Because her eyes aren't here anymore. Like in death, she was locked into a still-life of herself: a portrait of Joella, that still tends to lay out people on themselves. Wondering where she is, wondering if she is at all; and wondering how death can be so very final. So very, very real. It tends to slightly boggle anyone that attempts to reason with it. So they leave it be . . .

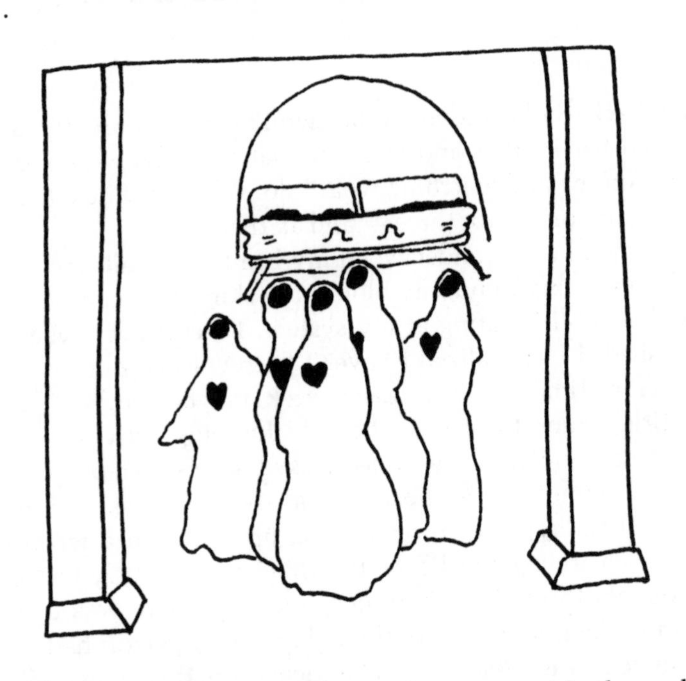

Bring back the incensed candlelit room with the radio playing something familiar. The snowy, lonely nights; standing, staring through a smudged window, waiting for someone. Bring back the summers and the sweaty horses trotting peacefully home at dusk; the sun just sinking but still hot. Casting a brilliant orange into their manes when the wind blew. And tasting that beautiful taste of a whole day's worth of dust coating your fingers and your lips . . . Bring back the feeling of leaping, thrashing, powerful horses through the lake beneath us, throwing a wake as big as a cruiser's. The slight snort, the sun again catching the water as it drips daintily into tiny glasslets and then back to the surface again.

Bring back even the times of soul-captive fear in the back seat of a squad car, staring dumbly through the screen, not free anymore . . .

Bring it all back and fill in this empty life hole I'm in now. To replace these useless drug-eaten thoughts that I haven't escaped and can't escape even yet. Bring back . . . and I know it can't be.

I can taste everything I describe, I remember it so well. I feel like I could simply shut my eyes and put myself in almost any situation I've been in before. Anything. And I could experience the same emotions and smell the same smells. What for? Nostalgia. The feeling of being able to *label* an *emotion*. The combination of smells, sights, sounds, colors, senses, and deep-level thinking. *That's* real emotion. I've even felt so alive at times that I could experience a tree growing through the sod, the crust of the earth.

I have only a few choices left if I am to stay alive. I *must* learn to face things as they are. I *must* learn how to handle things, because unless I'm dead, there will always be something to handle. There will always be something to get over.

J. Donlan
January 18, 10:03

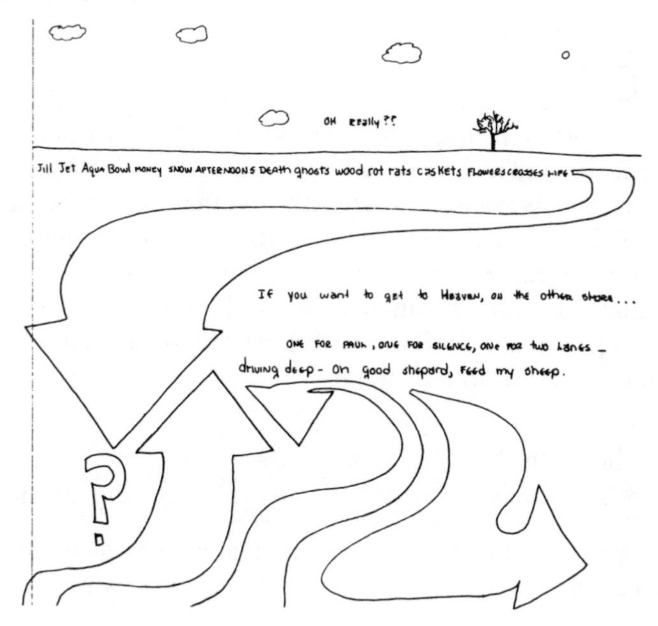

PROJECT JONAH: And then circling together this whole ridiculous day and realizing how morbid this person is because she winds up the whole thing with her name and the date and time, as if it will be the last thing she ever writes. But again I suppose, you never can know.

At least it's official, and again,

J. Donlan

January 18, 10:08

P.S. HERBALBODYBAR

January 20th

Man, acid is a destroyer, that's all. If anyone asks, I'll tell them right off. It destroys you very, very slowly and gets you high only because it's eating at your brain cells, and your system is in shock. It's just like dumping pure acid into your blood and feeling your body sizzle. It's bad. Very, very bad. I don't believe, at least with me, that everything is so beautiful with it. Everything is distorted — moving — foggy. Everything hurts.

It hurts. It's bad. It eats your brain. So I do it. Somehow I don't dig my friends doing it. I don't like to see them hurt. I'm different. I'm already gone.

To whom this damn well concerns (Parents, Brother, "Friends") or any other assorted Jesus Freaks and messiahs:

To put it straight, I do not trust any of you anymore, which is fair, because you don't trust me either, which is also fair because what you doubt in me is an extreme underestimation. In similar words, I am a lowly, unpredictable peice of street crap [junk], affiliated with many unmentionables, including pushing, stealing, lying, using, and very soon - maybe murder. But you must also understand, this is my best way to communicate with you because: you're not supposed to be in this [diary] and of course deny any such thing . . .

But if I do ever have proof that you've been looking through any of my things, including notebooks, old and new, diaries, pockets, drawers, etc., there is *just no way* that I'm going to stay around. Call it a threat, for what it's worth. I feel my privacy being threatened. Or even blackmail . . . There's one thing that I do demand and that's my privacy . . .

Love (if that's an accomplishment)
Soani — Joan — whoever the hell I am.

Acid Ha hahahaha . . . No, that's not what. What I mean either or something. It's like it should be that I'm back here with someone that's maybe or maybe not going to kill me with a gun only. Too bad. It might be kind of neat to be a captive. A big captive. Or a captain too. That might be nice. This is the third or fourth time I've had to sit here because I couldn't move. In a white room with black curtains. Oh shit. I didn't just go home and now I'm in trouble and I know it but I shouldn't be. Mother just called. I could if my pupils would shrink. I could. But I won't because it's blue out. That gave me a feeling like I'm waiting for the wagon . . . or . . . no! Are the pigs coming? I don't understand and—I . . . do care. I just wish I could what remember and that when I wanted to see Kevin earlier he had been around. Why wasn't he around? I wanted. Now they're playing "Changes." There are too many . . . Wow, smile . . . If I must die, that's how it will be I'm sure. Now the white petroleum jelly looks like patrolman jelly. Hey Kevin come get up here and be real. Be very real . . . Will I be? Dammit, Kevin, help me . . . Get up here. Where the hell is your God? Can't get no none of nothing. Too odd. Remember . . . haha . . . flew out like a . . . something . . . brain losing track . . . hahahahelpha

. . . lose it ? What you take you don't get back. Back . . . back . . . back . . . don't. Go back and grow better. Better. Don't get back. No Never.

January 23

I got a job at Country Kitchen, and like Roy said, I suppose that means I'll have to stay straight. I'm starting Monday at 5:00. I got another eighteen bucks today, don't ask me how I manage to get the money. If I tried this hard to get money for my bank account, I'd be rich. But as soon as I get it, it's gone on dope, and so am I.

January 24

Holy shit. I am really screwed up. Brent Wiser got my head (or what remains of it) kind of whirring and sparking through the charred ruins. Dan and Brent sat there looking at me, telling me they cared, telling me and asking me what I wanted to do, slamming me down and slapping my face and gouging deep. They hurt me bad. I wanted to do nothing more than cry. It was just like a funeral. I would have, but Dan was there and I would never try to show emotion near him anymore. He and so many other people that really think they're tough shit and use "Brent Wiser's method" of being critical and a together person and really don't know what the hell they're talking about. That ticks me off pretty bad. They seem to have a superior shit complex. That I just can't take. What am I doing to do? Get high? Not tonight. I'm high already. But . . . I am going to do whatever these old friends, the razor blades, want to do. Pain is all I need to level the hurt I'm having.

Through window panes trickled with tears,
I look . . .
I become what they mean to my well-hidden grief.
For a moment I feel the tears
rolling out hopeless,
releasing my darkness to drink its relief.
But the people around me do not seem to care;
they know they will see what they
know should be there . . .
And the rain, it kept crying my pain
from the sky . . .
The clouds locked in nothing.
I wished they were I.

January 25

What an all out bummer. Mrs. Donlan has been standing in my doorway for about seven different time periods and I can tell you, she's got me damn angry. I understand she's going to put me in St. Vincent's Detox. No, I won't go. I don't give a shit what happens to me, and I'm not going to waste precious time being straight and unhappy in a starch ward for any amount of time. I realize that I'm burnt out badly, but frankly, Scarlet Eyes, I don't give a damn. No more. They can do whatever the hell they want to do to me. They can sell the horses, and if they do, I'll make them very sorry. I'll kill someone. I don't give a shit about people. Or death. Or anything. Too many people, too many fucked-up ideas. Fuck everything. Beautiful. I ain't going to let anyone touch me. I'm happily dying. Very slowly. And believe me, it sounds very good.

God, there's just no place to hide. There is nowhere to go to get away anymore. Dope will do it, for only awhile. A very little while. Downstairs makes me have to talk and think because Mrs. Donlan is there. Upstairs there is only this room. This room has only cigarettes and music, darkness and somehow, a loud silence. Nowhere to go. No place to hide. No decisions. No mind to decide with.

I like dope. It is all I want. I want to fight and rob and steal and run, run, run. I want to kick and jump and kill. I want to destroy.

January 25

I've decided this school is really a pit after all. It's a real hole. Yuk. It gets harder every morning to wake up quickly, if at all. This school in itself is wasting my mind. Here I sit all day. Skipping classes, so far behind I could never catch up and I don't really care . . . so tripping is the only thing to do to keep my mind occupied. It keeps it full. I think I should leave. I really do think I should pick myself up and leave.

My mind has got to do something. It's got to think even if the thoughts are deranged a bit. Survival is the word and that's what I must do. Survival. Keep my brain and my body going even by artificial means. Like CPR on a person who's not breathing. It's only temporary, hopefully. And I hope it will drag me through these times with something left to go on with. If not, I have nothing left.

What I must do now is get totally bammed off my ass and burn out my brains. I do believe that I've never seen that much pot at one time in my whole life. Wow. Just wow. Very soon I should decide whether to go to Detox or not. It's a long time though, too long. Know what I'm thinking? Too long without dope. Too long without real people. Too long without the horses. Wow. Never seen that much pot in my life!

These people here at the high school understand me and the rest of us. If you trip and fall in the hall, no explanation is necessary. People just know what it's like.

Oh God. Time is distorted. (The table's moving) Everything has a green tinge to it. All the lines and stuff. This food is tasteless and sometimes I forget to chew it because I forget it's there and when I swallow it feels warm only and rather like it's pulling my brains down my throat. Controlling. Yeah. Open for control. Life force driving me to hell.

January 26

The police radio had me worried that Roy might be hurt. Then I thought it might be Kevin, and that's no problem because "only the body dies." HA. Cleaned barn. Brushed Seiche. Went riding with Sadie. Know something? They want to know who I am. Oh no. Here I am. More or less. TWO EYES, A NOSE, TWO EARS, GLASSES, FRECKLES, ETC. DAS EES WHO I AM. DAS EES. From the outside and I really don't want them or anyone to know who I am. Maybe. Maybe that's just a cover-up for the fact that I don't know who I am myself. Because obviously I don't. I look forward to summer but almost with fear when I think of surviving another winter. Another day. Have I changed so that other people notice? Or is it only that they expect me to change and ask me these questions that imply that I have — hoping maybe that my answers will be chock-full of what they want to hear? What do they want to hear?

SWEET DEEDLE DEE OR HAPPY FACE?

OH WELL, WHAT THE HELL!

January 27

I don't think I've ever wanted anything more than this: zip. There just isn't any. Mom figured a way to blame it on herself, as usual. "Did you know that I was on amphetamines when you were born?" See, she's trying to pull it off that I was a born speed freak.

January 28

I went to visit the shrink. The test results were apparently easy to read, and they said I was hostile, lonely, confused, unable to think coherently, and afraid of the unknown. Either bullshit or reality.

St. Vincent's has a 5 to 6 week waiting period, so I may forget it.

I returned Cris' call. He said he heard I got a job. I asked him from who, and he said, "Kevin."

Then he said he's talked to Drs. Wesly and Donovan and he asked me if I know they were both Christains. I answered yes, he had already told me that. He said they both believe, after talking to him (Cris), that quite a few of my problems had to do with Satan. I told him, yes, he had already told me that. He said both of the doctors were willing to attend a deliverance if I ever wanted to again. And so "just that you know we're available. . ."

Jan. 29

THE TIME IS NOW AT HAND AND I MUST CHANGE. I MUST SAVE MY LIFE.

Maybe, maybe only, Dan and I are still O.K. with each other.

I'm going to Detox whether I want it or not. I told Eric that I could start work tomorrow. I shouldn't have said that maybe. No more Bible study. But anyway, maybe that's alright. I wonder if I should go to One Way camp this weekend. Help. Goodnight. Tomorrow I have an appointment at 9:00 with someone from St. Vincent's. The carpet people are measuring my room and it's a pit. I want to fly. I need money for wings.

Jan. 30

What a dumb ass. I just cut my arm and it looks like track marks. Sadie writes:

"Remember no Friday parties at the hospital. Have fun, lots of laughs, good luck, you're going to need it. Good-bye. See ya soon?"

Mitchell writes:

"I think I'm going to shoot you. Be too rowdy in the hospital. Have fun. Bang, Bang."

Well, I have everyone's blessing. Except, of course, the North Door occupants, who just tell me, "You're one of the gang, take it easy . . ." and give me a hug, a pat on the back, a sympathetic gaze. I called Det. Reddy first. He said he was busy. Then I called Roy, and he said to take it easy. Then I called Brendan. He had time to listen. He told me to *"write him a postcard, drop him a line, stating point of view, indicate precisely what you mean to say, You're sincerely wasting away." [John Lennon, Paul McCartney, When I'm Sixty-four.]* He said he'd get hold of me later this week.

I don't know how I feel exactly. Yes, I do. I want to go on a trip. Acid, that is. Now. I need to pack. But I don't know whether to go or take off once I get that way.

Decisions, decisions . . .

Tomorrow is the day I should be bringing Joella some roses. I won't be there. It rips me apart worse than anything else may ever.

I won't be there.

I just realized how ridiculous an inscription on a gravestone reading, "It'll shine when it shines" would be. Pretty useless eulogy I'd say.

Know what they do to horse thieves?

Tomorrow is as tomorrow will be
Today is now and today you may see
Yesterday's dreams left you scarred and alone
Come take my hand and we'll both return home.

Please tell me I'm crazy

Still Jan. 30

I keep asking myself if I know what I'm doing here. It is January 30. And I think Mrs. Donlan has forgotten that . . . rather she thinks I've forgotten what this day means. Well, I haven't. I should be at her graveside today. I should have brought her a wreath of yellow roses. Instead I can only dream of doing that, and lie here in a hospital bed. I'm in St. Vincent's, for the record, and my roommate is an older lady, (she is sick, but she seems nice.) Room number 611. I have a phone, and they forgot to put a hospital bracelet on me and I realized just now that I could take off and they wouldn't even realize it for awhile. My head is really starting to beat and I'm feeling pretty logey. I think fairly soon I should truck down to the coffee shop and pick up some cigs. I may go crazy otherwise. I just don't feel like talking to anybody on the phone. I can only picture Seiche, Cinnabar and Spatts. Out in the snow free. I'm going to miss them. They didn't even search me yet. Hell, I would love to be tripping about now. I could be. They didn't take any blood tests or anything. Just the usual chest X-ray and vitals. I just got here. Hell, I gotta leave already. This place is making me confused.

It's somewhere around 7:30. I called Sadie, Cris, Turd and Dan. Dan was working and wasn't home. This is driving me insane. I think just this atmosphere makes me want to get stoned.

I feel out of place and kind of plastic. (Incidently, they nailed me with that bracelet, bless their little hearts.) Mom made me feel super guilty. We were only in admitting and she told me that this would cost $4,000 and we didn't have it, as it had to come out of my college money, so I probably wouldn't be going to college, and our insurance company would probably drop us. I think I have to keep in touch with this paper or I'll really flip out badly.

The woman in bed two has something wrong with her back. A disc or something. She's cried to every person she's talked to on the phone since I've been here. I do believe her that it hurts, though. Somehow I feel obliged to her as an ex-candy striper. The strangest thing is that my ankle is starting to hurt like hell (I think it must be only memory). I have gotten to think that this evening time period between dinner and sleeping seems longer than any. Food tastes like cardboard and makes my stomach turn. Something drives me to write in here. Self-preservation, maybe. I could dig a razor blade or two about now just to relieve the old habit. Seems like the whole white of everything here would be nice drenched in a little blood.

I spoke too soon. I never slept one minute last night. I have no idea what time it is. A nurse came in early and said she wanted a bunch of tests on me. Then I had this dream that I was here and there was a narc that used to be a pusher. Then I had this dream for sure . . . and Roy introduced me to the Mason County Sheriff who was a real short-tempered dude. There were some hawks flying over the field and they turned into big green dragonflies. They were flying low so Mom, (who was behind the barn in the Scout) attacked them as they were eating on the ground. She ran one over in the Scout by the workshop. P.S. I was so high I could float along the ground horizontally. I mentioned something to the Sheriff about the star of Satan, and he wanted to know why the star represented the devil. I answered him, "It's on your car, isn't it?"

A nurse woke me up and took five cylinders of blood out of my right arm. Now I'm dizzy as hell. Just now I have to take three pills of something with warm water. Ish. My breakfast came late. I still feel like shit. My doctor hasn't been in.

Jan. 31

What the fuck am I doing here! Son of a bitch. This is really a wierd trip. The whole program ain't gonna do me a hell of a lot of good. As Tommy would say [from "Tommy", by Peter Townsend] "I'm not gonna take it, never did and I never will." I don't get it at all. I just may try my hardest to get the fuck out of here. I don't belong here. Locked doors and keys and PEOPLE. Fuck it all. I ain't fucking chemically dependant. I've been a week or more without it. I can stop any time I want to. I'd rather live like a junkie.

Sat., Feb. 1

I am at Detox. The windows are locked. The doors are locked. My mind did the same as soon as I walked through these doors.

> long hallways——dark people.
> grey light——hold tight.
> locked doors——closed minds.
> empty hallways——people——light——minds.

As soon as I came in, the counselors gave me a "monkey suit" (or a pair of hospital pajamas) and took my street clothes. They told me I had to "earn back" my clothes because wearing them was a privilege and that I'd have to deal with my problems in group before I could get them back again.

Later . . . I would do anything to be free of this place. I can bitch all I want and knock people around and punch pillows and make them all happy. But I won't be doing any growing. Just shrinking. Back into myself. If this is what turns you on, it's cool. Not with me. I don't know what to tell them when I say I don't belong here. Speed was only a problem because I made it that way. I won't really get better here, because I have decided that. I've taken enough shit from other places. "Satan made you do it. You're posessed. An evil spirit. Trust in the Lord. The Drugs made you do it. Who is God? Abnormal . . . don't worry about what she says. She's insane." Faults/blame . . . Fuck.

I can tell you why I don't belong here . . . I don't need dope. I see things in my room. Maybe not. Who the fuck do you believe?

IT'S GETTING BETTER ALL THE TIME . . .

BULLSHIT. I am going to get out of this pit somehow. Those fucking pills make my head spin. If I'm going to be locked up, I want it to be in closed quarters. Maximum security. Bars on everything . . . Bars. I like people my own age. I've got so much on my mind. Yet I'm tired of thinking.

I saw you soar
you had no wings to fly
I know you saw
yet had not eyes to see
you think that you know
the height of your sky
but why not the high
of who you can be?

Sat., Feb. 1

Fairly soon these people will become ticked at me. I don't blame them. I have never wanted to die this badly. It wouldn't be hard. I don't belong here. I don't belong at home. Like I've given up everything. I don't even care if I get my clothes back. It's worth that to me to keep my feelings in. I'm not afraid of feelings for what they might to do me, I'm afraid of really talking to anyone because then they'll know how really bad my head is. I don't want them to put me away. I have to be free. Unlocked. Unsupervised.

My biggest fears now are that if I speak up in group for myself, they're going to think I'm bullshitting because my feelings have no meaning. They can change suddenly, on and off. What I THINK I feel has no pertinance to what I DO feel. I can't remember what I said only minutes later.

They'll only confront me and because I refuse to tell them anything, they'll hurt me. I don't have control of my thoughts or actions anymore. Just now I paced the halls for no reason and I don't remember a thing I thought. Please tell me I'm crazy . . . I don't want to be a junkie. I hear things that just can't be there and I see things that just can't be real . . . but so many people swear by them and so many say it's not so. Nights are miserable. I can't sleep at all. And I get so scared of my head and what it does to me. My hand turns into a white spider. Once last night I felt like I was dying. I was so very happy. I got the feeling that if I were terminal, I would have much more courage. I could let people hear me because they'd listen, knowing they'd never have another chance. But life is a terminal disease anyway. What the hell. I wonder if I just set my will to die if I could. No one's ever died of sadness except maybe hamsters. Having to face myself is too real. It's like going into surgery and not knowing if you'll come out or not.

The doors are locked tight;
you can't see through them.
The windows are clamped down;
you can't lift them.
The hall is short, the glass panes frosted.
The key is hiding on someone superior.
And five stories down the people walk
and breathe and run and sleep . . . and sometimes sing . . .
They don't need keys.
They're alive . . . and they take for granted their songs,
five stories down, from my white night.

Sun., Feb. 2

No group today because everyone went to church.

Freedom is easily forgotten when you have it;
freedom is best remembered when you don't.

Fuck it. It's alright if people leave me alone. If they don't I can't handle it. Locked up here with a bunch of stir crazy burn outs. Locked up here with myself. I am just writing to keep sane . . .

I just read some pages from my old blue book. It didn't bum me out. I don't think. Know something? I don't think I'm going to make it out there.

Instead of being in touch with my feelings like I'm supposed to be, I feel like I've lost them and they have been clouded or screwed up and I just can't lable them. I've gotten worse since I've been here.

I'm not going to group tonight. Too many people that care. The thing that hurts is lying to the people that I love. And being hassled by people that do it because they love me. That's pain. That hurts. I'm tired of words. Feeling, scarey, bullshit, caring, loving, guilt, hurt, lonely . . .

They all mix together and don't really mean anything anymore. I thought it was much earlier than it really is now. I look hurt because I am frustrated. I can't talk to a group of people. Not about what's hassling me really.

Child grown back from walls
comes sinking harder still
to take a rest upon her past
but finds it sealed and dark and cries
at the empty days that her age must paint
so that her life can be more than highways . . . leading where?
Streets grown up from walls
go seeking deeper still
to find a resting place along the way
and finding only streets . . . she sighs at her
empty mind
that only memories paint and make her life more
than just narrow alleys . . . leading there . . .
Woman caged with walls
goes running nowhere still
to vainly search upon her steps but
finds them old and weakened—she
dies from the empty painted days that
make her life more than just boarded stairways . . . leading
there . . .
leading where? ————
She grows old again.
The wall grows young from age.

Later . . .

Group turns into a colassal bullshit. I won't tell them. At least what I tell them is true, and more believable than the big problem. There is no one here that could help me with my problems with the unknown. What the fuck am I supposed to tell them? Now I can't tell one person what I feel. They write things about me on charts and show them to the parents. If that's what it comes down to, fuck 'em then. I can't trust any of them.

I don't have the right to be cared for. I NEED SOMEONE THAT WILL JUST SIT AND LET ME CRY. I need a good shoulder. When I cry I think of Joella and that's all. Barb just came in here and fucked me up royally. She thinks she's right. It's my fault that she doesn't understand. She's getting a report on me for the charts. I won't listen to them because I know they're wrong again. If you listen and you know you're right, all they do is confuse you more. So if they confuse you and you're wrong you can't be right because they're superior and they know what they're talking about.

That really makes me sad. Very frustrated really.

Since I don't feel I can write in this anymore without

someone confronting me on it or without someone reading it, I really am feeling, or I think I'm feeling, a lot of different things. I am threatened about my privacy and my emotions, and I'm angry that I'm threatened. If they'd let me be, I might burn all of this. Just like me, really. I'd rather destroy myself than reveal myself. Robert was only giving me his opinion. There are really no standards of how to live in this world. Only that you're happy, and sometimes not even that. I've listened to these people so much that I have my head saying yes and no to life itself. Yeah, well maybe, but I guess not, never, but someday, I don't know, of course I know . . . it can go on and it does.

Feb. 4

I am really pissed off. Because I'm different and don't really dig playing Foosball or cards or whatever, they put me down. Tell me who I should be, tell me what to feel or that I must feel something. They critisize me for what I like, they dump on me and tell me not to dump on them. They tell me I look pissed when I look them straight in the eye and try to read them. They're telling me I'm playing a game when I act the way I feel. I must be screwed up if I come across that way.

Debb made me make a contract to only write in this private diary for one hour each day and I tried to mingle but there was just nothing at all so I decided to sketch Seiche and Debb stuck in her head and said, "Oh, by the way, that means the drawing book, too." So I shut my eyes and really jammed some songs in my head and fell into a dream right away. Lauren is here. She screwed up in Treatment and she is being shipped to treatment in Georgetown tomorrow.

Some will, some won't. You never can tell. I've got a fried brain, really spacy. I'm gonna fucking choke myself while I'm sleeping without knowing it. Or flip out and jump out a window. I feel desperate. I feel out of touch with my mind. Going slowly going once fast spinning slowly out of control.

Feb. 5

I'm scared. I feel threatened. I feel mad. I don't want to tell everything about myself to group. Not everyone wants to talk outside of group. I do. But screw that. What am I getting accomplished if I scream and yell? I'm not satisfied with a hoarse voice and a headache. I want to say something so that I can come across with what I mean. Maybe I don't know what I mean and that's why it seems like it's all a game. To me, group seems like a play on people's emotions and nothing more. The counselors and the kids are all mad at me because they think I'm playing a game. They'll ask me if I want to deal with it. I'll say no. They say I'll have to take a risk sometime. I'll say yeah. They'll say I'll have to take a risk if I want to get straight. I'll say I don't want to get straight. They'll ask me why I'm here. I'll say I'm waiting to be put somewhere else. They'll say where and I'll tell them. And they tell me it's bullshit.

That's the way it goes. I get threatened of not being believed if I say how I feel. If how I feel sounds right they'll tell me I'm people-pleasing. If I tell them how I feel when I sit in my room and what I think about, they'll say bullshit-you-just-want-attention-you're-playing-a-game. I won't take that. It's too frustrating to try to explain to them if they don't believe me before I open my mouth. I came here to get away from home. I came to be alone with my head so I could think straight and write. I had no real idea of whether I was going straight or not. I still don't. I don't dig falling for that bullshit. It's just like the exorcisms they've done on me. I get the feeling that they don't know what the hell they're talking about. I am reluctant to even listen because of what listening has done to me. I am hurt, scared, and pissed off. Some of the hurt is from a long time ago. The fear is from knowing I'm getting worse here. More hurt is from being labelled as something that I don't think I am because of my fear to talk and have them find out that I really don't belong here, but somewhere else. I hate this place. If I say what I mean, I'm afraid that they'll stick me in an institution. I don't want to be crazy. I want to be very free and I want very much to get rid of the thought that the only way I can be really free is to be dead.

Thursday, Feb. 6

I have mainly been writing in my big notebook, but only for one hour a day. Last night I earned my clothes because I "dealt with my shit" (what was hassling me) I got jumped on by everyone and I just couldn't take it anymore. They broke me. But the feelings that were there were put there by the group. I admitted to feelings that I didn't really feel or at least have contact with at all. Robert has always scared me. Tonight he started hitting me with a pillow across the face and calling me names.

He threw me a pillow and told me to hit him. Everytime I hit him he hit me harder. They laughed at me at first because I just stood there and took it. Then Andy came over and held me and told Robert to stop hurting me. I was grateful until I saw he was just mocking me. That did hurt.

I just had a one-to-one with Robert. He left me crying in the O.T. room. I wanted to tell him so badly about the people that told me I was posessed and how much they still scared me. He walked away.

Lucy and Robin were just in here and I told them about the exorcisms and I shouldn't have. Then they get afraid of me and I don't want them to be because somehow that makes me different. If I were in a group right now someone would confront me and say that I'm trying to be different by being a loner. I like caring for other people. I can't care about myself because I don't give a shit about my life and right now I feel very, very trapped and forced into my gut feelings. There is no way around it anymore and they hurt you if you don't deal with yourself. I like to have people be O.K. with me. People get super pissed at me if I be the person I have been for a long time and still want to be. They put me down and tell me I'm only conning them all and they're really pissed because I'm only playing a game.

They hurt me when I be myself. I know I haven't known who I was for a long time. Maybe I am unconciously screwed in the head. I almost wish they'd put me in isolation or something. I can't even see out the windows. The frost is in the way.

Another crisp morning
through the glass and the screen
from the blizzard that has died
and left the fancy cars
buried to their hubs below

Another day in isolation
giving me something
to work with in my thoughts,
a gift
to have a window and light enough
to watch the policemen tag the cars
along the alley
where the ambulances come screaming (I
don't watch them anymore.)

WE WERE MEANT TO BE ALONE
TO KEEP HURT INSIDE —
WHY DO THEY TRY TO FIGURE ME OUT?
WE WERE MEANT TO MOVE FAST ON THE OUTSIDE —
HOLD OUR PANIC IN OUR HEARTS.

Another winter morning
in a locked room
five stories up from the cars and the freedom
I begin the slow climb from the mutilating, tattered life
to one where I can face the pain,
and at night
when I wish I could stagger
away from the others,
feel the frost bite my nose,
watch the world fuzz into darkness —
the frost comes
and paints my window
with lullabyes
and stories
and silver nights . . .

Sat. Feb. 8

I wonder, most of all, where I'm going tonight. No, see that's the kind of thing that I'm afraid of. I just wrote "tonight" when I should have said tomorrow. My mind has been wandering. It's like getting broken-in to jail. I'm slowly adjusting to the rules and the jobs and the occupational therapy and the whole general schedule. I could be lying on my couch in my room now, afraid of being called a junkie by anyone. Afraid of being called depressed.

I can picture the red light, the remains of an altar. I wish I was there. But when when I think of the feelings I'd have by being there, I'd get high tomorrow, I might be high tonight, and the day after tomorrow I might be dead.

Sometimes I feel like running away. Growing takes pain and courage to deal with your feelings. I've almost made a dare to myself to get tripped when I get back. It sounds really stupid to half of me, alright to one quarter of me, and Satanic to the quarter that listened to Kevin.

I was nearly sure that I was together as a Christain. I don't know now. I hate myself for not accepting my parents' love.

Sun., Feb. 9

I went to Church. Because it's Sunday, we have radio privileges. I sketched a picture of Robin a moment ago. Charley and Farlin are in here. I find it sad when nothing comes out on paper but daily happenings. I can't write like I used to. I want nothing more right now than a good hit of acid. I can open my hand and imagine there is some zip in it. Or some purple micro-dot. I've been living in my head all this time; afraid of my emotions. I know I feel hurt, but I don't know why. I am here. Locked inside on a beautiful day. Hopeless in a sense. It can't do me any good if I don't want to go straight. Sad because of Joella, and other things that I never did get over. This day is definitely fucked.

Feb.10

What a bummer. Locked in here with stale air and a cold bug floating around. You can't escape it once you get it, and there is nothing to take once you get it. That's where I stand right now. This morning in group I had to leave because I felt so shitty. I had to take some tests for the shrink. Erik said I should lose my clothes before I left group. I did.

Robin and Charley left for treatment. I ran out of stamps. I'm beginning to feel shitty again. I made Tom a belt in O.T.

Howdy Sis,

Hope this thing hasn't got you too bummed out. It's for the best, really. I would like to see you do your part to solve or work on your problems. It is really hard to keep giving and trying to help someone (even through professional methods) when you don't get anything in return. Remember these people do give a damn about you and their way of caring is to help you. They can't do it all themselves. I would like you much more if you straightened out and cared about yourself. It is hard to love someone who doesn't care about herself. Mom and I are putting together plans for your room. So far all the wallpaper she's brought home I thought looked corny; no funky stuff, and I've yet to see a good looking piece. We'll get it together though. Thank you for the belt. It's really outasite. Try and get wheeling on doing your part for you. You deserve it.

Tom Donlan

Feb. 11

I had orders to call my mother during morning group. She said she doesn't want me home until after Treatment. She said the shrink told her I wasn't even sure if I wanted to go straight or not yet. She said she and dad were both mad. I think this is fucked but I can't go home. RUN. The doors don't have to be open if you're desperate enough. I'm serving time. If I run, I'll be caught by the pigs and brought back here. I came thinking two weeks at the most. I've been cheated.

Dear Joan,

First of all I want to tell you that I love you. Maybe more than anyone in the world. (You know that.) And I want you to be happy. If I have contributed in any way to your present condition

. . . like getting in the way of your growing up — I'm sorry. But I can't undo what's passed. So let's get on with it.

I'm tired of worrying and hand-wringing! I resent having to take care of the horses! I'm tired of having my throat close from one panic after another! And guess what? I'm wrung out. I'm not going to let it happen anymore. Until you can make a decision to do something about yourself, I've had it. I see no point in coming to the parents' sessions at the hospital. Why should I try if you won't? Maybe you need to reject us altogether to find yourself. You'll never have a better chance to find out who Joan really is. And you're blowing it. I refuse to live anymore with the worry and misery of trying to understand and handle your problems . . . especially now that I know you've been using dope. Home will only be here if you straighten yourself out. Only you can do it. I can't solve that for you . . . and neither can anyone else.

There will be no living at home until you get out of the chemicals. Once you have made the decision to stay straight again, we will support you all the way. You really haven't leveled with anyone . . . least of all yourself, I guess. Things won't get better until you do. I told you that your "being possessed" doesn't register with me. I don't buy it — never have. You don't need it. You have control over that, too. I'm through trying to find your answers. All I know is there aren't any answers in the phoney world of the doper. You're on your own.

Mom

Dear Mom,

We do listen, here. And I learned a lot here. And in a way, I'm glad that you're standing up for yourself. I refuse to take responsibility for your feelings because we also learned here that you only feel what you want to feel. In other words, you made yourself mad or hurt even if I was the main factor. In either case, you didn't have to get mad or hurt. That was up to you. I see this program as having done enough already for me now.

If I went home now, I could easily stay straight. I didn't come here originally to get straight in the first place. I came here to find value in myself by having a clear head forced on me. I feel that I've been tricked and conned a bit, as I'm sure you do.

You can know because I'm telling you, that I respect my feelings and thoughts and judgements so much that I can only reject the people that persist on me talking.

It makes me very angry to have things written about me in charts and report forms and recorded on cassettes. It makes me even more angry when everything I say up here is reported to you. Their method of "growing up" isn't cool with me.

About being possessed. Listen, because I'm tired of explaining it. The first real risk I ever took in group slapped me right in the face. You may or may not have talked to Cris about it.

All I know is that it happened. I can't choose to believe it or not, because you can't understand the unknown anyway. *It happened.*

There's nothing more I can tell you because your mind's already made up that it's all a big "game."

If you think four or five hours is a "game," or ________

Just forget it.

Wed., Feb. 12

I don't give a shit if I find out who I am or not. Leave me alone.

We had a special group tonight because some people thought that Robert was coming out sideways with his statement about "some people losing their clothes unless they shaped up." He got attacked, and he looked either pissed or helpless. I didn't think it was sideways because I haven't been working in group myself, and anyone else who isn't should know it. The others didn't agree, but I told them my opinion and I stood up for what I believed in. I wanted to give him a hug when I saw him at the desk all spaced out and hurt looking. I wouldn't work through my fear of being rejected. All I did was tell him I really was sorry and that I didn't like that attack at all. I am less scared of him now than I was before. He's actually human. It freaks me out that a counselor is actually human. I cared enough to cry for him. If I told him that, he might tell me that he doesn't need anyone to feel sorry for him. I do feel. I cried for him.

I've been hearing a lot of people up here that are doing something for themselves. They talk about their parents, their love for them, and their tears and their anger, and their futures. Their feelings. I hear them and I want to cry. I'm sitting here (that's my fault) and as usual, I'm being left behind. Everyone seems to grow but me. Again, that's my fault. I can deal in group, but I wonder so much and my head has yes's and no's flying at my mouth from all directions and my memory is screwing me as far as group goes. I forget so much that it seems like I'm lying when I say what I think I feel during group. I just talked to my parents. They both had tears in their eyes.

Thursday, Feb. 13

Last night Margo called to say hi. I couldn't talk to her, of course, but it was nice to know that she cared enough to call. Either that or she was stoned enough to call. After a while, I retreated to my room and turned out the lights and laid down on my bed. I was spacey and I felt like crying but I didn't know why. I guess Debb believes I have to hit a "bottom line" before I decide to go straight or not. She thinks my bottom line is death. I've thought about it for three years and I guess I'm not afraid anymore. They want to know why I'm not putting anything into group anymore. I don't know. If I went home right now I could go straight without anyone's help. Just from listening, I have learned enough to get by. I know what they say I have to do to get straight, and I know I can do it all, but for me, I don't agree with their methods and bitching at a punching bag tends to screw up my head.

I'm hurting tonight, but almost afraid to deal with it because I sense the group really is pissed at me and will hamper rather than help even if it's unconciously. I can't be sure what happened to the group after the old gang left. There are so many new patients that I'm losing my trust. I feel alone. There are so many hidden feelings. The circle is really tense. The real love, and the real caring seems to have been lost.

I really care for people here, but all of us together can't seem to trust each other. I don't understand.

Ed just walked up to me and gave me this poem. What *serenity?* What blessed timing!

Oh, what serenity —
what blessed serenity
that comes from
trusting someone enough
to let your thought be known —
knowing a gentle mind will
pick out the good & true,
and with a breath of kindness,
blow the rest away —

Sun., Feb. 16

I feel myself changing again. This I really don't understand. I say, like Donovan, "First there is a mountain, then there is no mountain, then there is."

> Sunshine waking, have I made you cry?
> Do your tears burn hollow holes in the sky?
> Is there any way I can help you through?
> God knows, I've been dreaming too . . .

Mon., Feb. 17

Yeah, this place is just like everything else with me. I'm behind again and it's my own damn fault. Tomorrow Farlin's leaving and then I'll be the veteran. I've been in detox for EIGHTEEN days now. A few people that came in a week after I did have gone. I'm bumming out. Cindi and Ed and Peter left today. The first went to Treatment: the last went in a pig car. Johnny Be's leaving for Treatment tomorrow. Three new people have already filled in the beds.

I don't want to talk to people. That's my only decision. I like being a loner and I like keeping most everything to myself. That is my business. They would tell me it's my own problem. Artful Dodger came over from Treatment and really bummed me out. He's bummed me out ever since I first saw him up here. I don't understand. He keeps asking me how the devil is. I finally asked him why he was saying all that and he just said, "Well, you're the one that's telling all these people about this devil shit." Then he walked away. What the fuck can I say? I've been through it. I guess my past experience with the Satan worship is really getting in the way up here. I don't have any desire to live at all. I don't care anymore. I can't even talk to these people about it because they don't know me. I fucking didn't know until it happened to me. It's so unreal. There is no way around the fact that it happened.

Tues., Feb. 18

Shit.

(later) . . . I have more to say than that. But there's nothing I can do now but cry.

Feb. 19

Yesterday I narced on George and he is being discharged tomorrow. It was all such a big scandal. He got some dope from some chick when we went down for a lecture and brought it up. He was ripped when we got back. He said he could get us some more if we wanted it. At first I was excited. Then I got real scared. There were other people; new people that hadn't been here as long as I had. They hadn't given their heads a chance to clear yet. By letting him get them high, they'd be discharged, and in the long run they might end up dead. I had to give myself a chance, too.

There are people in the group that knew almost as much as I did and are lying about knowing anything. I'm really in touch with a feeling and it's very strong. I am really hurt. It hurts so much that my stomach gets sick. I want to cry very much but not alone. My trust has gone downhill. I feel close to Andy and that's about it. He gave me a hug last night and told me I would be alright. I haven't heard that in a long time . . . at least not when I almost believed it . . .

George left about an hour ago. They said if we wanted to say goodbye we would have to hurry. There was a sheriff transport man waiting for him. I got to thinking, run, George, run . . . but I guess that's what he'll be doing in one way or another for the rest of his life unless he decides to change. No one said anything to me or even looked at me. I felt blamed. They were silent when he walked past me. Through all the goodbyes and pats and handshakes and hugs, all I could do was shrink back in a corner and soak it all up like a sponge. It was like they were all blaming something on me. I was ready to show them I'd changed this morning. Then it seemed there was nothing I could say that would help any of the people. There was not one word to say; not a question to ask. Erik got down on me and told me he'd like to see me leave. From there on I was really speechless. It makes me think my brain is screwed. I have nothing to say. Robert thinks I'll end up in the psych ward. I just frizzed my hair. Must go to sleep. Liza has her lights out. 12:35.

At parents' group, Dad said he was proud as hell of me. Fuck. I'm not proud of myself at all. Half of me says to screw this pit, and craves to hit the streets again. Another part says, "Keep going, ride with it. Get straight." Another part says it's too late for any changes but death. I don't know where that part of me is coming from. They just want to back out of myself. What exactly I will do I don't know. If I go home, it's right to the streets again. It's right up to thirty whites a day, and acid every night. It's right down to a slow, gradual, but evident death. If I die, suicidally or the other slow suicide, I have nothing but my fear of the unknown. Heaven and Hell. Heaven or Hell. Or nothing at all. There can be no proof anymore. I don't care what these Christain organizations say.

Now they tell me they won't let me go. I'm locked, scared, and facing even more of what I thought was as good as dead — myself. They were going to put me in Glenhill. Then they could just nicely tuck me away. But I would be there for a long time too. I don't want to be here, I don't want to be there, I don't want to be home, I guess I'm just going to have to be somewhere I don't want to be. Seiche is going to be affected by me and so is Cinnabar. My family and friends too. How can I change them so much? What makes their lives so ruined just because I do dope? After all, they're not sick . . .

Why should I, after this, even consider my own life when these ruined lives are everywhere because I changed? And because I decided it might be nice to try a little of that white cross, "just once?"

Baby come home
love us like you learned how
smile and show us
that you never really changed
laugh and tell us
that this was all in sleeping
hug us and smile like you know how
Go to church, late for school, wake up . . . touch your feelings . .
Baby come home to us
We do love you, for now
we won't have you
Because you're not who we promised ourselves you would be.
For now . . . You're not smiling like you should be
We love you/we don't want you

Only for awhile until
you show us we weren't wrong
in hoping for an angel
Baby come home . . .
show us how you can smile . . .

Joan,

I want to tell you how I feel. I wish I could tell you all this by talking to you, but I'm not very good at talking, so I'm writing it. I love you. And I miss you. And I'm as mad as hell at you. I'm angry at what you're doing to yourself. I'm angry that you won't help yourself when you're surrounded by people who are trying to help you help yourself. I'm angry that you won't listen, and that you're playing games and conning the people that are trying to help you help yourself. I'm angry because you're angry with me and won't tell me you are. I'm hurt because you won't tell me how you feel. Or write me how you feel. All this anger and hurt adds up to the fact that I'm damn unhappy. Not with what you are. Just with what you're doing. I'm unhappy because you aren't facing reality because you can deal with it, and you can't deal with what's unreal. I'm unhappy because you have made it impossible for you to come home. You have. Not anyone else. You. I'm unhappy that you're thinking about running away. Anyone can run away. Anytime. I can run away. You can't run away from yourself. I'm angry because you aren't putting your guts to work to help yourself. So you know I'm angry and hurt and unhappy. I feel you are, too, but you won't say it. And I'm frightened. Scared. Because reality says you don't care enough about yourself or about those who love you to let you get help. That's scarey.

You won't get Treatment. You can't get into Fairhaven if you need to for two months. You can't get into a foster home because no one will accept responsibility for someone who's irresponsible. So what is there? There's Georgetown and Cambridge and Zimmerman. State Mental Hospitals. For a long, long time. If you don't think that could possibly happen, you're going to be surprised. That's not a threat. That's what happens when you act the way you do. I'm sore. I'm ticked. I'm steamed. And it isn't going to go away until you do something. Do something for yourself. Don't tell me you're going straight. Go straight. Now.
That's what I feel. Anything else is B.S.

Dad

Feb. 21

Another note from Mom. She doesn't want me home. She says she's sure I'll end up at Georgetown State Mental Hospital. With the people that moan and crawl and make animal noises at you just like in Hell. A note from Dad also. The story's about the same. They moved me into the isolation room today. Liza left and another Peter came in. My hair worked alright. My mother could not look at me during the lecture. She saw me go by and she grabbed Debb and started to cry. Home to Detox. I read both letters again and cried from 9:00 to 11:00 all alone in the dark of my room. What am I going to do? I don't need a mental hospital. I'm as sane as anyone. They won't let me go once I get there; I know it. I could be there for years. Like Roy said about someone else I know. He's a loser. I can't help him. Nobody can. He'll be in and out of different institutions for the rest of his life. How am I so different from him? I'm caught. I feel like this is all a bad dream. It scares me. Why can't I just open my eyes and wake from it and leave it to its hell? Everyday it just wears on and my thoughts don't really change. But I'm not insane. I'm not brain damaged. They'll sell the horses anyday now. I just know it. Maybe they'll move away; out of state, and try to forget I ever happened to them. Maybe they'll all die. It scares me also when I think I could be myself and talk in group if they were all dead.

It revolts me, disgusts me, and turns my stomach to have my parents being told almost everything I say. It makes me sick. I could expect anything right now. Anything could happen. Tomorrow Brent and my parents and Tom and Dr. Gilbertson will decide what to do with me. It won't be home. There's so many places I could be going. Why didn't I just run and never come here behind these locked doors? I can't see myself escaping before I'm eighteen. By then I'll be committed. I'm trapped. There aren't many ways out.

Part three

Locked, scared and facing myself

How many years until I'm free?

I don't even want to write any letters to the old gang because they're just chippin' away back home, thinking this is all a vacation. I couldn't begin to tell them what a nightmare it all is . . .

Feb. 22

It's only ten minutes before group and I am already on edge. Notes here and there about my parents calling about me and someone else stopped to talk to Robert about getting me to talk. Joan this and Joan that. No participation, no motivation, nothing. Just looking out the windows I realize that the next place I'm in may have bars covering them. It scares me. How long am I going to stay trapped? How many years until I'm free? It will be the rest of my life. All this; the beginning of an end. No hope. Fear. It is impossible for me to go home. How many years from now?

• • •

It's after lunch now. I just finished reading Revelations in my new Bible. I might make it after all. I have definitely turned to my higher power. I know the first step. "We admitted that we are powerless over drugs and our lives have become unmanageable." I have to admit that. Now I'm lost and they're going to lock me up and throw away the key. My god, it's my life! My life is slipping under.

• • •

Just ate dinner. Robert told me tomorrow night my parents and I are going to have a meeting. That's it. Fucking firing line. BANG, BANG. You're dead. That's right. I'm dead.

• • •

It's now 11:20. I'm scared, like I'm shaking. I don't think Robert likes me too well, and I don't blame him. Dodger came over with the interview people and he really was disgusted with me. He asked me if I was pulling that "Satanist bullshit" here and if I was trying to be like Tom. It ticks me off.

Sometimes I go into group wanting very much to talk and before I can get into things someone will say that I'm just sitting on my ass and then if I talk, they'll nail me for complying. I'm blaming them and that's not cool. I don't know what to say for feedback because I don't want to hurt anyone. There's just nothing. I'm afraid, deep inside, that I might be crazy. I don't want to feel things for other people. I can easily show my feelings to the kids in the group, but I'm afraid of the counselors. Probably because they're right about me sometimes. All in all, I know I have a lot of pride. It gets in the way. Paula left tonight. She's in treatment and Adam just got accepted. I'm so fucking scared. *Damn* scared.

• • •

I feel like I've got gut rot. It's around 1:15 on a Saturday morning. I wish I could flash back to any day but today or any time because these days have obviously been the worst days of my life.

Feb. 23, Sunday

Got turned down for Treatment. I'm hurt, but it's not because of all that. I'm so unsure of myself that things seem distorted. They tell me I've only been playing games and I don't think I have been. I don't know when I'm being real or not. I change so very quickly and I don't remember what I said or what other people said and it sometimes passes and makes no sense.

12 Steps of AA
First Step:
Finished in Detox, Sunday, February 23. Wrote out explanations for each effect to check out my chemical dependency. *WHY AM I CHEMICALLY DEPENDENT?* My main reasons for deciding I'm C.D.

The love I felt for my dope was overpowering. I'd wake up in the morning and think of my favorite moment of the day; first coming to school, hitch-hiking to avoid my family (or if I needed money, going in the car to get "lunch money" from Mom) and walking directly to the north door to get the pick of the morning's dope from the dealers, or selling mine when no one had any yet. I reached into my pocket often to hold my bottle or stash whenever I felt insecure. I felt powerful and able with dope in my pocket; without it, I became lost and hopeless. Being preoccupied took up time for anything or anyone else. My family fell apart, school, friends, work, the horses, the cops; everything was affected. I admitted I was powerless over the drugs and my life has become unmanageable.

Second Step:
I am at the point now where I believe that there is some type of higher power that can help me, but I'm reluctant to accept it. With my background in religion, I was driven to reject God and Satan and totally keep them out of my mind. But then — I think back and compare "coincidences" from the past and I've come to believe that God wants me here, because now everything else is shaping up too, outside of the hospital. It almost had to be planned, because if this works out, my life will fall together as it should.

I've rejected God and thrown away chances to learn about Him and believe in Him, but then I have to ask myself: Why does whatever I do become involved in some way in Christianity? Why did I go to Bible study at all? Why did I happen to be signed with Kevin for the ride-along program? And why did I get refused but learn who Kevin was and what he really believed in even after that? And why did he happen to be a cop? It's just all too perfect. I believe that a power greater than myself can restore me to sanity if I accept Him.

Third Step:
Tonight, Tuesday March 4, 1975, I am turning my life and my will over to the care of God as I understand Him, hoping that He will guide me and help me fight the war for my straightness here at St. Vincent's and on the outs. I pray that He may show Himself to me through people and other things

every day, and that He will also help me to say the right things to them. I pray that He will remind me of the consequences of taking dope ever again, which is insanity, death, or suicide. For these reasons, I hope that the war becomes worth fighting always, and that I should never become so discouraged that I didn't care about dying or living. I pray that God will take me from here on, with my help, too, to keep me clean. I give Him my life because that is the most that I have, and I have proven in the past, I am unable to cope with it. This which is my greatest gift of all, I have nearly given away. The two things that will help me now the most are my life itself, and God to guide it, day by day.

Feb. 24

I'm really mad at Anne. She's just sitting in the corner playing her attention games. There's a lot of that going on. It's bedtime again. I'm making a bridle for Seiche in O.T. This is strange. All the chicks are pairing up with guys except Kathy, and she's the horniest of them all. I wonder how my real Dan is? I am so lucky just to have him. To have anyone; and I treated him like royal queen shit. I loved my dope and I loved him when he was doing dope, and suddenly he changed . . . or was it me? . . .

Feb. 26

I got really bummed out in group today. Anne and Robert asked me if I wanted to go straight and I said, "For sure." They asked me if I believed that. I said yeah. They said I was being compliant. What the hell??

• • •

I know I'm here. I know it was wrong to start doing dope but I did it, and I might die without this. I'd rather hide back in myself, and mingle among all my secrets that I love and hate and gaurd so well. I say I can be happy in my own insane little world of past things and I believe it. Without control over my emotions by use of a pill to make me glad, or a pill to bring me down whenever I choose, I always go to the things that have made me feel things in the past to feel things now. I need an excuse to feel. I am scared because if I really feel, they might reject me. Alone. People do funny things when they're alone.

The cat with a gust of wind and a
smile from his face and a shadow to hide in
goes by and slinks with a message of bad news;
a message of death . . .

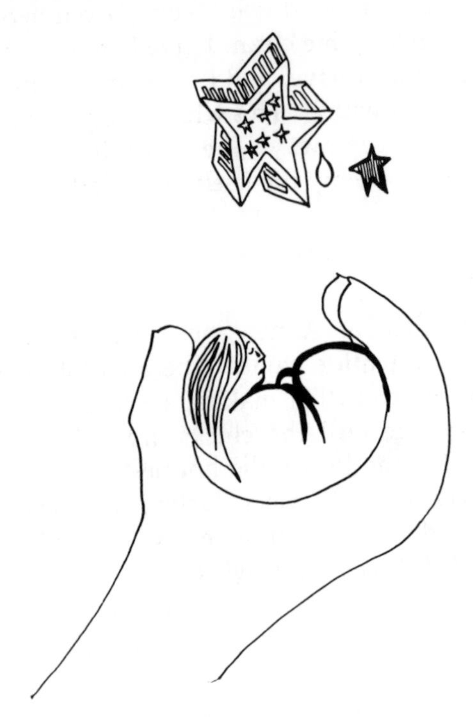

On Surrender

Night will come eventually.
Do not have expectations
for today if your evening is falling
before its time.
Stars will face the early dark
as you might know they should.
However far they seem to you,
never doubt their constant changing.
Dark will soon enough take back
the mornings of your grievances.
Do not give in to dwindling hours
or void a simple tear.
Night may fall tomorrow from
what burns so high today and once it comes it won't return
or leave a sun for rising.

I'm on my way, I know I am

Feb. 27

This is my first night here in Treatment. Last night during parents' group I was reading my old junkie notebook. I don't understand why I seemed so happy and together. It's really been bothering me. Maybe I shouldn't be reading all that, but every so often I wonder how I felt then and what I was thinking, and how I dealt with things (if I did at all). I wrote to deal with my thoughts and feelings, and I got high, and I talked to cops that I had taken for friends . . . but I never really dealt with my feelings to myself; for myself. It hurts when I see how blind I was. Some things I did I still consider morbid in a funny sort of way. I don't understand if they were only that way because I was stoned or not. It seems to me that my writing is less interesting since I started going straight. Then again, when I did my acid I couldn't write at all, and half of the time I didn't want to. There is no way to talk or even prove that you're a human being on acid. I never even made sense to myself. I used to sit and mumble that I "didn't know, I didn't understand, and I didn't care." But I did care somewhere deep inside; and I hid from everything else.

Dear Shelly,

I got your letter. You wouldn't think I'd be busy up here, but I am. I was locked in for a month, and I just moved over to the drug treatment center where I'll be until April or later. Anyway, it's too boring to go into details about this place, so I won't.

How's Big Mike's going?

You're lucky to be out there and *free*. (You're also lucky that I'm not around to shoot cap guns at you or pound on the windows.)
[Unfinished.]

Acid Nightmare

Purple drips down from my eyelids
and coats the dark hall in wet watercolor
but I am not crying
as slowly it paints my nose and my chin;
or falls a short distance ahead of my face . . .
I only am flying;
And windows become fountains and filter the sun;
a darkening pinwheel that dances and taunts . . .
the sky breathes its sighing.
My mind joins the chanting and may become lost,
a spiraling rocket that spits and chars . . .
so far from my dying . . .

Mar. 1, Saturday

Last night I called Dan, after asking for my concerned person privileges, and everyone O.K.'d it. The conversation went something like this:

"Is Dan there?"
"Yes, this is Dan."
"Dan? This is Joan."
"Oh, hi."
"Guess what?"
"What?"
"You got voted for my concerned person!"
(silence)
"How's Artful?"

And he told me he had been getting high. He told me he didn't know if he was dependant. He said he was tired of all my letters and all "that bullshit." He said all he had ever considered our relationship to be was just a friendship type. That really fuckin' hurts. I felt, when he told me he loved me all those times, that I couldn't be sure of my feelings enough to tell him if I loved him or not. But he did tell me that, and I don't understand.

I have heard it before. It's not the first time, but I thought for sure this was real. He cared, I think. But he did the same thing. I was used and now I'm hurt again. I had a one to one with Cat and I cried a bit. In group tonight I dealt with it, but somehow there will always be a memory there.

Whenever I lose my way like that, it hits me hard and I get hurt. I must begin to work on the anger involved. Artful's friends did a concert here for his 17th birthday. I am lost because Artful's leaving soon and I need his support and I'd like to get close to him. We both have lost Dan for the meanwhile.

"It's all over," said the enemy that once had been a friend . . .
"We've taken all we can," he said, "You'll have to start again.
"Good-bye," someone answered in a supersonic voice.
"Because you still won't listen, then I guess we have no choice."
So the winter turns around again; I wonder where I'm going . . .
I've lost a few and found a few, but I miss only one.
And if he'd only hear me I could let him know my mind. It isn't much to give him, but it's all that I could find.
So, good-bye, I love you, keep the laughter in your eyes . . .
Good-bye, I love you, I'm trying not to cry . . .
Good-bye, I love you,
God, show me that you heard . . .
I screamed, and woke in silence . . .
and he hadn't said a word.

Johnny took off and came back tonight, and I lost my clothes because I wrote my job on tomorrow's list instead of today's.

I called Tom and he really didn't want to do a concert here. Gave Andy a goodnight hug, gave Erik a goodmorning hug, and last night Robert gave me his style of a hug (strangled headlock). I am scared of tomorrow. I miss Artful and he hasn't even gone yet. Finished the noseband on Seiche's bridle. I long to be homeward bound. It's up to me, but I will be.

That fear of being lost in the downward spiral is still there. I can see myself walking around all bummed out again, and if I got off after this I'd probably kill myself at the shame and guilt and self hatred. Went to AA downstairs. Gave Artful a really good, secure hug. I should go to bed.

It's 5 to 1:00. Day by day. I have to remember that. Keep working.

"I'm on my way; I know I am!" — Cat Stevens

the city street at night
under flowers of neon
over fields of asphalt . . .
my home tonight
the wind through the alley
between my enchanted forests
of buildings upon buildings
beside more and more
just like trees I've seen
but you can't look past them
you don't see around them . . .
my house tonight
the bench in the park
like a boat on a river
of trash and sand
pray it drifts swiftly away
from this place as I sleep . . . I pray it's not
my bed tonight . . .

Sunday, Mar. 3

Ed just confronted me in the hall. "Pony, you seem to have been walking around in your own little world for the past four hours." I never noticed. I want to go home, but again I don't. I guess what I'd like would be for me to be in a situation like I was before, minus drugs. Tonight I'd be riding Seiche down 13 towards home. I've lost contact with the reasoning behind all of this.

• • •

Something is going on inside of me tonight. Artful is leaving tomorrow and I'm scared because I want to go too. I don't really feel close to anyone but him. That's what I'd like to do tonight. I'd like to run tonight. I hate those permitting open doors. You have to trust yourself so much more than in Detox. The doors are open, the lock is in your mind. I'd like to walk around and breathe real air. I'd like to see the bright lights and feel the winter air breaking into spring. I want to be able to sense things. I don't care anymore. I think maybe

I've been conning myself. I was never aware of it, and maybe I'm only imagining it, but I don't think I've changed. I don't like this. I'm lonely for my old self. I want to be alone, but it's against the rules. I lost a good friend Friday night. I have to think of him as dead. It hurts, but I'm tired of crying. I want to be alone in a field where I could lie deep in the wild oat grass and cry outloud. Just to lie and dream.

While it Lasted

While it was there,
        it was fun . . .
But it won't ever be again.
Not ever. Know that.
It's got to end sometime.
It does, you know.
It won't ever be the same again.
Not ever.
Hello lonely . . . scared . . .
It's got to be that way, stay that way . . . forever.
Feel that.
Smile if you feel it . . . or lean on me and cry.
We know what it was,
    and we knew it had to end sometime.
It has, you know.
It had to.

Find Another Stone

Find another stone.
Throw it at your feet
when you find it.
Break it on the earth.
Open wide the ground.
Find another rose.
Throw it to the earth
when you find it.
Smash it in the grass.
Find another stone.
Throw it in the air
when you find it.
Break it through the clouds.
Open wide the sky.
Find another rose.
Fly it up and higher
when you find it.
Let it dance upon one star
and then
another . . .

Wednesday, Mar. 5

Down and up again. I may be alright. I may not. I want to go home. I finished Seiche's bridle. Gave Robert a goodnight hug. Family group lasted until 11:00. I wasn't in that group. Washed some clothes today. I studied the Steps last night. I must believe in what they're saying.

"Queen?"

"Yes, I'm still here."

"Do you understand love?"

"Love? Of course. Love is helping people and talking a lot and thinking and going places and going there — fast."

"Definitely. Just like love is cement bridges and iron girders and fallen stars and cities . . . right, Queen?"

"Definitely."

"And hate?"

"I wouldn't know the answer to that, now would I? I don't hate. I help you . . . And you help me. But this Treatment you're in won't make me go away. I'm here. Anytime you ask for me I'll always answer you. And you and I both know what the answer is, right?"

"Goodnight, Queen."

"Goodnight, dear. I'm waiting for you."

"I'm not fighting you, but I won't do anything more than accept you. I must go now . . . "

"No! Wait! Don't leave me up here all alone. I get scared too. I get lonely . . . "

"I'm sure you do."

"Do you care about life?"

"Yes."

"Then why are you locked into yourself? You gotta hit the road. Let your mind roam. Not anymore?"

"Not your way, because I don't want to die. Not under a bridge . . . not in a field, not even in a library. I don't want to die high anymore . . . "

"*I* will."

"No, you won't unless I do. You're part of me. You've lost your royalty, Queen. Your throne is being smashed. No one will be sitting there anymore. I have to stand up now. I have to leave you."

Thurs., Mar. 6

We did commercial skits instead of group. We went out for a walk this afternoon. I haven't smelled fresh air since January. I got my rowdies out. Family group. Tom came. I think we're O.K. Mom told me Kevin thought the house was being burglarized because he saw a ladder on the side of the house — and when he stopped in, he said he might like to come in and see me. Brent Wiser came and gave me a good "go-out-and-eat-'em-up" talk that helped me a lot. Tom brought me my Cross. Mom got some hay delivered.

Sun., Mar. 9

We went to Terrance College to play Foosball and boogie to the music. Dad came and we talked really well.

Mar. 9

Ward 5A.C. We all live on a mellow 5A.C. — mellow 5A.C. — mellow 5A.C. . . . Mellow enough to get everyone's clothes taken away this morn until tomorrow morn because no one woke themselves or anyone else up. I am in bed with something; I wish I knew what. My face got hives after my shower and then Linda and Joseph called the resident doctor. I don't know what it is, but they just took some blood out of my arm.

March 10

I just read through and counted the pages in my old notebook. All of the hours and days I spent thinking I was doing something "constructive" and writing things that made good sense . . . It's just more than a hundred pages of nothing. Not a thing worth keeping. Just like there ain't a thing worth living for with dope, except one more day to "experience your mind" and to get higher and higher until you're totally out of touch. This is what I have to accept about myself and this year. It was all for nothing.

March 11

I don't understand the things I do. Whenever I get in touch with a feeling, my thinking goes absolutely insane and that scares me. With hurt, usually all I can think of is Joella. Some tell me that's a cop-out. They say I'm not being real and looking at what *really* hurts. When she died, it was during a time where I was very withdrawn and fairly insecure.

My grandfather died on the tenth of the same month, but I never did really look at that realisticly. I knew he was gone, dead, but (I supposed) happy. When Joella died, it was a complete shock to me and it scared me to think of someone young that I had talked to only days before being totally gone and just seemingly disappearing completely. Where did her thoughts go? All we saw was her body, and nothing moved. What happened to her dreams? Her ideas? What was everything that happened before worth to her if she was to lose them completely so soon?

It scared me because I knew there must be something left of her still. Some spirit or soul, and a higher power to take it on . . . or something. Face it. I don't understand death. I'm scared of it because most of the time I feel like I'm being watched by all these people that have died. I can sense it. Like right now I know there's something else in the room besides myself and Ruby, my roomate. I can just feel it. It's always with me and it has been for two years. I don't think it would affect my sobriety at all, and maybe it doesn't get in the way at all, but that is how I feel about it and I still do have feelings about it and maybe I always will.

Maybe I don't want to forget. No, I have no control over forgetting a thing like death, a thing like *that.*

But I don't want to be so scared . . . It sounds so damned insane to anyone else . . . I try to get in contact with the reality of a death. I visit Joella's grave, but all I remember of that is the way it was on that February day, two years ago, at her funeral.

Wed., Mar. 12

Whatever they gave me for those hives today didn't help at all. Maybe I'm just allergic to the water here or something. My old babysitter, Kitty, came to visit me. I'm dizzy and sick and those fuckers don't believe it. They think I'm just making it all up. I think I should just shut my mouth so they won't have anything to laugh at me for.

Mar. 13

If I go back to dope again, eventually, I will be dying. I know that at least, because I knew that when I was using. I knew I was dying but I didn't care. It seems almost impossible to talk about how I feel because people here are judging their knowledge of me on the charts and on all the bullshit I did in Detox. They say I haven't changed. Sometimes my thoughts are so insane; so scattered, that I feel inadequate to even open my mouth. I don't want to get into a psych ward because I don't need it. When I read this over it doesn't sound real to me. It must be, because I felt it.

Fri., Mar. 14

Love doesn't seem to get anyone through anything up here. Fucking scandals and secrets and jiving. It's got me defeated.

I sometimes wonder where the hell I am. No one's serious about their lives. After all, that's what's at stake for all of us and we're nowhere near the safe road home yet.

I've been praying lately that I could accept people's love and care and get the help I need to live on the outs. I want to be free; I don't want to be stoned. More to the tune of: I want to be high, but I won't be. And for now, because of that, I can't be free either.

Spring

I am not as the winds outside this window have become to me
    I am not anything as they are
I am not as the sun on the puddle of melting snow on the street
    I am not quite that bright inside
What I am is all these together;
stagnant, waiting for spring . . .
  as the flower clutching the deep, waking earth
sleeps silent also, within my heart
  These are what I have become . . .
with the changing of the seasons . . .

Today on the way we saw a death cart wheeled by. Funny, the sort of silence it brought on . . .

Death cart roll by me still and silent
  down the hall,
holding a body that maybe I could have
  talked to before (maybe I have).
  We could have
shared some secrets or just
held each other and hoped for morning.
  Death bag zipped; stretched tight, scalp to toe,
teases in a loud whisper of its lifeless cargo . . .
  roll by me quiet and call my name
(yesterday maybe, but not anymore).
  I feel the presence still.
I sense a silence that laughs at the world
    all the way down the polished hall,
Leaving some words in the air as it passes,
  "I know what you will soon . . . I know . . . I know . . ."

Very Free

I think of being free again
I think of open doors
      they stand before me
      and behind me
I think of them as locked
and they won't open
      for me until
      I'm very sure
      what they lead to
I think of snowy nights
I think of dark roads
and they haven't gone forever
   they lie ahead of me
I think of them as lost
I won't return there
    until I'm very sure
    which way to follow them
I think of being alive again
I think of all I've missed
    that hides behind me
    locked behind me
I think of it as dead
and it makes me sad
    that it won't change again
because I'm very sure
of what it leads to
and of where it ends . . .

Mar. 18

At first I was sort of afraid of Bill, because he was so right on in group. Whatever he told me about myself was so right. Sometimes that can get scarey. Rodney was so funny tonight after dinner. It seems that he has been studying Bill during his lectures and he's worked up one hell of an imitation. He kind of stoops over and motions with his hands and talks halfway like Donald Duck and repeats Bill's infamous phrase . . . "Mad, sad, glad, afraid, ashamed . . . " We've seen the same lecture so many times that we practically have it down in our sleep. — Ruby wants me to help her curl her hair. Gotta go.

compliant

defiant

guilty

Rowdy

spacey

elated

passive aggressive

content

scared

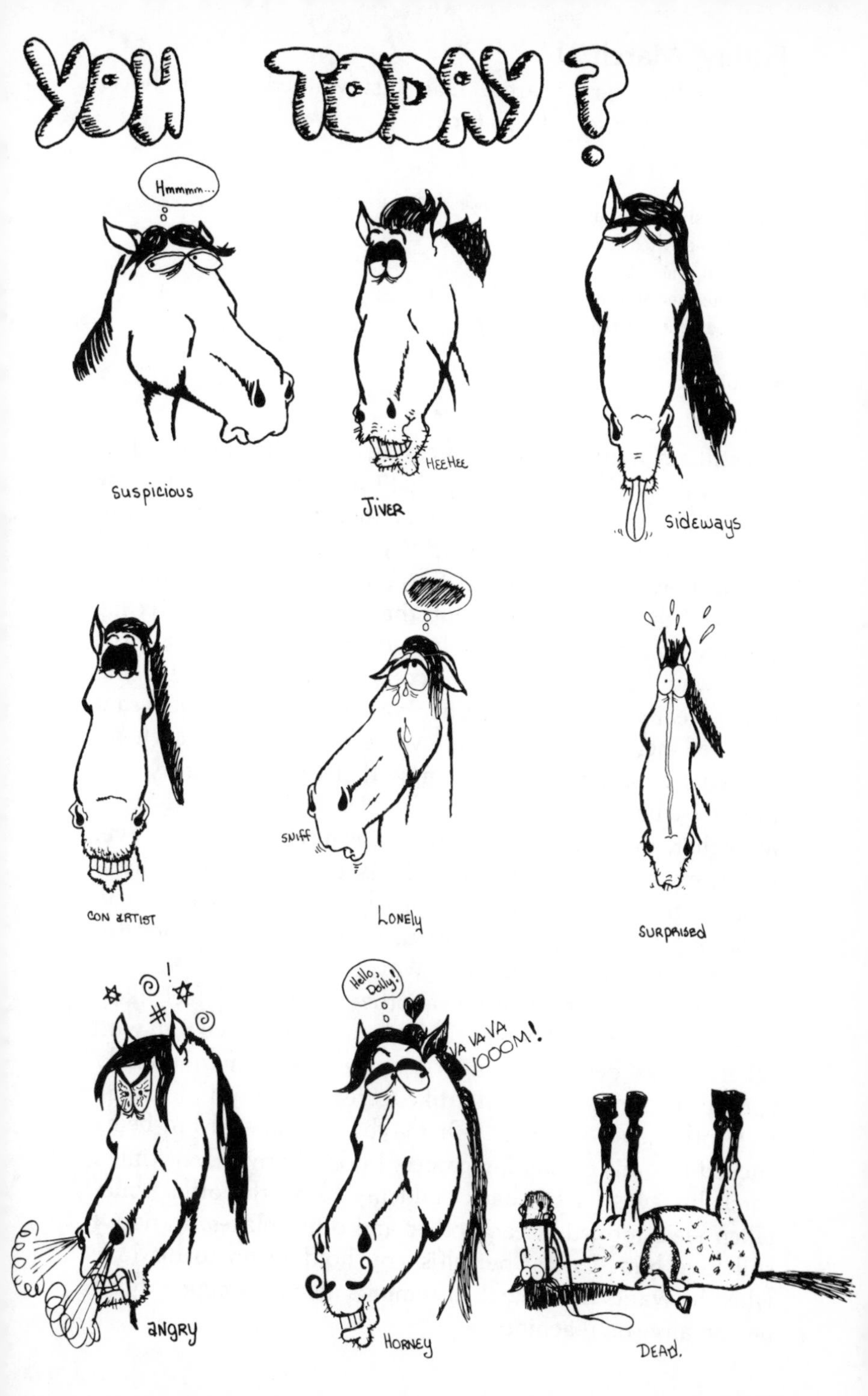
YOU TODAY?
Hmmmm...
suspicious
HEEHEE
JIVER
sideways
CON ARTIST
SNIFF
Lonely
SURPRISED
Hello, Dolly!
VA VA VA VOOOM!
angry
HORNEY
DEAD.

Friday, March 21

I am feeling very scared. Dan just walked in and he is probably in my squad. Oh fuck.

Why?

Why doesn't one of us
just tell the other one
of us that one of us
thinks neither of us is
really being us and that
one of us thinks that
both of us know it?

• • •

I still am writing. I want to cry again but it's not the time. One wall is the only thing that's between Dan and me physically. It hurts so badly that there's more than a wall between us in our relationship. I get sad when I see him. I realize how lucky I was just to have someone for as little a time as I did. He said in group that he felt a need to fix me because so many other people had broken me. He said the only way he could see me accepting help was by being really, really close to someone. He said that's why he'd said he loved me. I guess I was only vaguely aware of that when I started seeing him. It hits me now that I was trying to "fix" Simon by being close to him. I wonder if I hurt him? Maybe after that, I thought of Dan and me as having an equal love. It was my fantasy. I lived what I wished it would be. I lived what it never really was. I still can't say I was wrong in dreaming that someone could care the way he seemed to. Things just don't work out that way.

I think he's started seeing another chick, so I feel like I have to stay out of his way. It hurts me when I see him with other chicks because I guess I realize that I'm not really special to him anymore. I'd like to feel that both of us had each other, but we don't. Or maybe we did and I'm being sucked into his explaining games. I don't know. Everytime I catch his eyes I flash back suddenly to all the other times when we'd looked at each other and other places. I know I still love him. I must be selfish by holding on to his love when he wants to shake it. It reminds me of keeping a dying person alive on machines.

I have to have the courage and the kindness to let go, for his sake. And mine, too, if this is all that's going to become of it. I can't talk to him. I can't even look him in the eye. I love him too much to ever start liking him — I can't be just his friend. How can I treat him like any other resident here? How can I possibly give him a hug and not remember when I thought it was real love? I see just no way. It hurts to reject him. And it hurts when we both avoid each other. Walk by in the hall looking ahead, at the floor, pretending we both have no feelings. My head is confused, but there is no doubt about what I feel. I feel like dying. I haven't let go of love yet.

Mar. 22

I have to accept that the kind of love that I dreamed we could have was never there as far as Dan was concerned. It was for me. I cried. Now I'm avoiding him. I want to confront him on this "avoiding" shit but I'll sound like I'm trying to "fix" our relationship. It's dead now. If it ever was alive or even existed at all.

Mar. 23

I finally had my one-to-one with Dan today. It was hard to see him avoiding me and vice versa. He won't admit to playing games with me at all, even though I admitted mine to him. He was playing games just by going along with *my* games. I'm sarcastic as hell and that just proves how pissed I am. I have to remember that Simon never meant that much to me until he was gone. Dan enabled me to be crazy, and I let him have a false love because he wanted to fix me.

He told me today he'd rather see me go to "7th floor psych or something." He lowered me and put me below him so he could talk to me. "I'm in treatment and that's all I need. But you're here and that's not cool because you're more screwed up than I am and you belong in a psych ward."

Mon., Mar. 24

Dan asked for visiting privileges for Chris Bains. His girlfriend. That hurts.

Siren wrote me that she had found a guy that she really

liked and was getting loaded. She said she was happier than she'd ever been in her whole life. I started my fourth step personal inventory and that hurts, too. Oh, fuck.

Mar. 25

What is there to say?
I wish I could have just one more day with you
and be together; just us, together again.
But you are here and I am there
and it won't change and time won't either
Not even my love can move the wall we have;
can break it down . . .
not even love can tear it away.
What is left to say?
I wish I'd had just one more day . . .

• • •

The guitar sings out, but it's only in my mind.
The guitar sang out tonight; and then I saw you
glance at me slightly and turn away when the
words sank in too deep . . . and I glanced at you and turned
away when the words burned in my eyes . . .
and the guitar sang out and spoke of love and loss,
of mountains and dreamers, painted ponies . . . and
stormy skies at night . . .

Thursday, March 27

Carl, the hospital Chaplain came up on the floor tonight, and instead of group we had our own "Last Supper" feast. He turned on some music from "Jesus Christ, Superstar," a song called "Look at all my Trials" . . . and he washed our feet and we all had Communion. I read a passage on the meaning of Easter. It was really deep. The sun was blasting Spring-red sunset across the room and it hit me as I read the words. For the first time in a long time I felt like God Himself was wrapping me tight in His powerful arms and saying, "Hey kid, I love you. I really do." And for the first time in a long time — I believed Him.

child slams hard into someone within herself
much older and feeling
someone coasts gently to the woman inside her
he told her his feelings
woman clings silently against his love unfolds her to the child
and the someone within herself, much older, has to know grief
before she can find love . . .

• • •

I feel like dying
because I'd like to cry
but the time is rushing by
and I'm supposed to sleep now
and feel my pillow against my forehead
and wake up with wet eyes and tangled hair and
an empty mind and
I need somebody
because I feel alone and I'd like to cry when I know
someone other than myself can hear me and
take care of me and
love me back quickly to fill in the hole
that the tears left . . .
but I'm supposed to sleep now . . .

First Step Review

1. Preoccupation: Many times in school I'd find myself thinking so much about drugs that I'd write poems about them, write schedules of my day centered around dope (buying, amounts, and money).

If I found myself in an uptight situation where I couldn't take the dope, I had an unconcious habit of reaching into my pocket where my bottle was, just to hold it. It gave me a sense of power and security. Eventually, when money ran low, all I'd think about was how to get more. I was scared, but the fear came not from the thought of my possibly being addicted, but from the thought that I might not be able to find any more. I hid my dope, but not very well. From my friends and parents, I denied having it or just hid it well when I was near them.

2. Attempts to Quit: I said I would quit last winter, but I was doing it so someone else would be proud of me. I wasn't doing it for myself. It didn't last more than a week. As soon as I got into speed and acid, I had no desire to quit. My goal was to die high.

3. Lying: When I was high especially, I'd lie a lot because I felt so good. The thoughts were coming fast and I was on a completely superficial level of reality. I felt like making other people happy, too, so I'd lie about something that would make them feel good. I even lied that I was going straight. I felt like I'd want to feel when I was straight. I lied constantly about my drug use to my parents, until I decided they knew anyway, and then I merely denied needing any sort of help. The kind of lying I did probably hurt me the most because I was really lying to myself and it could have cost me my life.

4. Kinds, Amounts, etc. I started taking any kind of pill that I could find and stealing some from hospitals. I saved up some from after my operation. That's where I first experienced a mood swing. Then I started drinking and smoking pot. It stayed that way almost until the start of the school year, when I started doing speed. My tolerance built in about a week from five a day to ten a day, then twenty, and thirty.

I did acid very often, blotter, four-way and purple micro-dot. At the most I did three hits of purple a day, and I sometimes went with one or two a day for a week or more. I did the zip everyday, usually mixed with acid, and occasionally smoked pot (and drank) on the same days.

5. Effects: I lost weight on zip, and it made me very shakey and uncoordinated. My voice and my motions were awkward. Acid generally burnt me out and sometimes I got very bad strychnine cramps from bad blotter. It made my muscles stiff and tight. I found it hard to talk. It made me paranoid and afraid sometimes.

6. Effects on family and social life: I had no social life but with my dope. I dropped all interests in people and friends and stayed with dope as the only friend I could trust. I resented family holidays or socials because it took so much effort to act straight and phoney and polite. I had no interest for my family and our relationship went down and apart rapidly.

7. School and work: I dropped all my classes, and lost interest in my work.

8. Spiritual life: It made me feel guilty to go to Bible study on Wednesday nights like I usually did, and I finally gave up on religion because I'd heard too much from both sides and I couldn't make up my own mind.

9. Character: I began to steal. I lied. I did anything for money or dope. I planned everything in my head. I was sneaky and enjoyed carrying these plans out.

10. Strange behavior: Hallucinations. Flashbacks. Black-outs. Violent behavior on impulse. Sudden mood changes.

Setting myself up to be hurt or beaten.

11. Destructive behavior: I thought about killing people or spiking their food, but I never did. I cut my arms with razor blades whenever I got frustrated. Getting so burnt out in itself was destructive.

12. Accidents: I over-amped a couple of times, walked out in front of cars without looking, lost all my care in doing things right. Never thought before I did anything.

13. Effects: *Financially;* I was carrying a lot of money that I got in various ways, but always, if I had money I didn't have dope and vice-versa. Paying for the horses was out. My bank account got drawn out, and now I'm broke. *Legally;* Just being busted for suspected possesion or being out after curfew. *Morally;* I threw away a lot of my morals. Now I think I feel mad about it but I can't tell.

April 1

Last Letter to the Queen: What can I say to you for all I know of you? I have known you for a long, long time. But I haven't really known who you were at all. In the grass by the road by the City Bank I on my horse once stood close to death either way. I come now and sit in the *same* grass and light a candle and smile at friends and cry at the wind. On the wall by the road we stand and look back and look ahead and never move and never plan to.

How can I see you when you left so long ago? In the night, in an alley, on a hill that still protects my memories, like a box with a tarnished spoon inside . . . locked tight. Dishing out past dreams, lost people, like an unmerciful killer. Relentlessly going on and on. Tomorrow by the wall again, or maybe on a hill; that hill. Why are there so many roads within my mind? Down one or two came a horse like a puzzle. A beast much like a picture from my childhood. Up one; down another. I kill some memories; some will kill me yet. Upon the lake dances the sun and like a cleaver swims the horse, the wake follows and he snorts.

How can I find you when you left so long ago? People tend to move away and travel far. You may even be close still, but there is no way that I can tell, and I will keep you in the tarnish of the spoon within the box on the hill. I must keep you there, and I can only think of you now and then. I have lost control of you in my mind, but I haven't lost you altogether — for all I know of you. I have known you for a long, long time. That's all. Tomorrow you may kill me. Tomorrow you may tell me it's alright when it isn't, and that is why you will never find me again.

Part four

Here comes the sun

I feel that ice is slowly melting

April 3

Snow, real snow under my feet! The sun is real again, and it's not temporary anymore. I still had to be escorted out (of the hospital), but I walked to the car on my own. What feelings. Everything is rushing by me . . . past, hopes, dreams, LIFE. I am like a small blind child who has regained a never-before-felt sight. And . . . I could think of nothing to say that would wind it all together, so for my crystalization talk, I wrote my thanks in a poem.

I'm going home tomorrow
still I think I'm out of time
The day that's left before me
seems already far behind.
It scares me when I think of where
I could have been today . . .
An empty mind, a hardened heart
with nothing left to say.
I'm coming back again. My life was only death, and then,
I'm here again — with so much more to go
Coming home to live, and leave what's left behind me . . .
I love you and I'd love to let you know.
The people smile and still somehow
I feel so very torn
To leave the place I think of
as the place where I was born . . .
The door behind will never close
but I don't have to hide . . .
Your love has filled the space in me
where part of me has died . . .
I'm coming back again, my life was only death, and then . . .
I'm here again — with so much more to go . . .
Coming home to life . . . to leave what's left behind me . . .
I love you and I'd love to let you know . . .

Home again, naturally. Went to River Falls to see Mike Johnson [in concert] with Tom.

Someone was toking behind me. I'm scared. Outpatient tomorrow.

A tapestry of all there was that never could be
is my life and it hangs and rots where I can't see —
in my brain all is sad and very empty
when I cry and I tell myself I'll make it but I
never really try
I guess there's nothing more profane than a life
that has no meaning
with a friend or two that only say they love me
in my dreaming
I have lied and I have hurt them then I swore that I
would change
but everything worked out the same with nothing rearranged
I've damned myself a million times
for shunning God above
but I need too much attention and I'm so afraid of love
I can see me huddled lonely where I'll surely always stay
While my empty echo dies its last, "Come closer; go away."

April 4

I have the whole rest of my life to get high if I choose to. Give myself a chance to live. I can read your face as well as I can read the time . . . and I know I have to go home. No questions are being answered. Nothing I said is being remembered, no plans are being carried through. It's all been a fucking set up. Goodnight, Joan. Damn it. It seems that nothing . . . not love, not a future, not people . . . nothing, can change who I am/was. What will it take for me to live and be happy too? When can it all change and melt away into another bad dream? . . . Until tomorrow . . .

Tues., April 8

High til I die, don't have to think. Don't have to feel . . . now wouldn't you say I've got quite a deal? High til I die . . . don't have to yell, don't have to cry, won't even know . . . when the time comes to die.

Last night I almost bought some zip. Got sensible, scared, and split. I saw Roy and Shelley at Big Mike's.

Sat., April 12

I mixed a drink and took it upstairs. I threw it in the sink and laughed.

It's so good to be able to do that. Joel says I'm testing myself.

Sun., April 13

Happy Birthday. Lonely out tonight. Torn. I don't want anyone to care about me. Happy sweet sixteen. Artful and Fred Contoree and I were sent on a treasure hunt all over Willowood. Roy Wilhelm helped us. It was ridiculous.

April 14

Lonliness can easily drive one insane.

I feel so into myself today. I see nothing in the way of getting high except myself. Daycare isn't doing anything for me. I see myself on a road going the wrong direction; on a cliff going close to the edge, on an ocean going under . . .

I am not, at the moment, making it at all. I hate myself. It's all getting refucked too fast. I wondered how long it would last. I'm supposed to leave it up to my Higher Power, but talking to someone who doesn't talk back seems like a lonlier thing to do than just talking to someone, anyone . . . even on a surface level. I walk around Willowood at night, this time alone. I've had to give up the majority of my friends and watch them slip by me. I've had to watch the dope take its toll on them all.

• • •

Now I'm sitting in the can at Country Kitchen looking at all the graffitti about me. Beautiful. "Pony is insane . . ." "Pony is at the funny farm . . ."

April 15

I've just taken the Talbot Starship [hospital elevator] up here to the group room. I saw Roy again last night and he asked me what had happened to me. He said I was all closed in again. I told him I didn't know.

"Well," he said, "Keep looking up."

"I can't right now." I said.

"Why not?"

"If that's the way I feel . . ."

"Well, fight it off . . . " He looked at his watch. "At the time it is right now, I doubt if I'll see you again tonight." He pulled the car into reverse. "That's the problem with having a cop for a friend . . . I always have to go."

I started walking down that damned road again.

Later . . .

No shit. I just walked out of Daycare. It's all over. Joel said, "Look at you, You're dead. Absolutely dead. Your body's all tight, your face is frozen, your eyes are fixed ahead. You're rigid. Dead." So he said he was pissed off at my game. And so was the group. He wanted a decision so I made one. Charley opened the door. Beth said, "Pony don't. I want to help you." So there I stood. Then I said, "Fuck it," and shut the door behind me.

The first thing I thought of was how to tell Mother. And the first way I thought of doing that was by getting high. But I won't. Why not? I don't know. And I don't care.

Wed., April 16

I readmitted myself to Daycare. I was accepted again.

Sun., April 20

It hurts so very much to rid myself of my old friends. Junkies especially for some reason. I am no one. Nothing at all anymore. I walk into an old crowd and I become the little-low-to-the-ground chicken shit that pulled out. I walk into a room with some old straight ex-friends, and I become the burnt-out junkie freak that isn't as much of a person as she was before. I run into an occasional cop-buddy (or ex-buddy), and I become the in-between, "what-can-we-believe now?" person. I am nowhere with myself.

> She who rules so many
> Has fallen, now, for one . . .
> Gold paint chipped from her plastic wings; she fell
> And brought down the sky.
> The Queen is crashed . . .
> But she was not killed in the fall.
> And if those who have left her return once again,
> They'll have no chance, no, no chance at all . . .

April 27

The horse show got rained out today. Rain, rain, go away. Dump on me another day.

Another day —
nothing new seems worth it on the
slate grey skyline
pressing me down, holding me from flying.
Another drifty morning that
somehow got away from me.
Afternoon again, and too soon
I'm wishing it were dark
and I'm hoping to forget the absence of stars,
crumpled in my shell.
The grey light floods the stable where I'm curled
letting my mind drift like the time.
A horse snuffles at my presence by his stall.
Another day —
nothing to say is worth saying.
Empty mind like the pale dead sky
pressing me down
holding me from flying . . .

Mon., 28

A friend got busted and I heard it on the police radio and I laughed . . . until I found out it was him. Help. I'm lonely with people and without.

I feel lonlier than I have ever felt before. Where am I going? Where have I been? And what am I doing here?

April 29

Daycare again. I knew it wasn't all going to be good after treatment, but being real is so painful sometimes. Do I have the guts it takes to die?

May 2

I was up at Big Mike's and I told myself I would be real there. I was not. It seems like I always have to impress someone with my little dark insanity. We got mooned. Roy drove up in the new squad car. It's ugly.

Sun., May 4

Wow, man. Just wow. Seiche won a blue ribbon in jumping at the show. It feels so good to be up there again. But I'd love him anyway. He doesn't have to win anything for me. Movin' up in the world, we are. Ha. Unreal. From street kid to Fairy Princess in three easy tries.

May 5

I got my new contact lenses today. I checked out school. My advisor said to check out getting a job instead because it wasn't worth it for just three weeks. Scared of Daycare tomorrow. What am I afraid of?

May 9

And he and I, as with he and himself, as I am also with myself, is older and I am too, alas. I got a job as a night waitress at Beek's Pizza. And I kiss my contacts goodnight, and boogie for bed.

May 10

I pierced my ears. Cherries took Seiche to the horse show. Tom's birthday. Why is tomorrow within itself again?

May 13

Daycare, then home for a banjo lesson. I'm not interested in banjo now. It was a thing that came from my junkie person. The colt got gelded today. It was kind of sad. There was power in owning a stallion. I was control over power.

May 15

No change.

May 18

Tom told me at the piano that I couldn't go on playing plain old major chords forever. Change, change . . . you gotta change! Run, keep pushin' . . . movin' . . . Change. Why am I moving so fast? Will somebody tell me why I have to keep on going? Why run? What am I running from? WHO AM I? I feel like I've been robbed. Someone has taken me away from myself. Where is my [old] room? The walls? The air? The darkness? The safe death? Where is that girl that was dying?

Mon., May 19

Hot . . . Tornado later. I went to work. P.S. I love Eddie Mcarsin on the bathroom wall. (Not me, I just like the graffitti.)

May 21

I went motorcycle riding with Roy. We stopped to see Cinnabar Foxe's dad [the stallion]. Cinnabar has a new baby sister just born today. I'm starting to feel like I belong in this world after all.

May 24

Stash's in Summit Treatment. I saw Kevin. He's had a spiritual awakening from having a wart burned off the palm of his hand.

May 27

I am paranoid about the times I had and who has taken them. Maybe no one has, but they are completely gone. The north door of school simply isn't as much of a mother as it was in the crisp, final depths of winter. The people are gone. They don't know me now. Did they ever know me though?

All they knew was the silent, hall-trodding, broken down, burnt-out and stuck up little freak. But that girl was part of me. She became all of me. And she is dead. She died as I walked twards the main entrance to St. Vincent's, as the doors locked behind me, as the snow left the ground. I see proof of her, and things here show me she did live. When I think of her, I long for her, too. I see her like a seperate person might have. She never cared about *me.* Yet she was a part of who I was. She is away again, head in the clouds, and she doesn't even know I have left her. She stands way above me and laughs cruely. And she lies in agony below, smiling morbidly up at me. Where is she really? She is in *me.* She won't ever leave. Nor will she ever grow any older than she is right now. Unaware, she was unafraid of death. She searched for a faster way to it. I have to stop this. Although it is all true, I have to remember; I would rather feel lonely than unreal.

Promised Land

Teddy bears and dragon flies;
I've found that they still light my eyes,
and days of never-ending song weave
lilac chains that reach so long they
hold the past in tarnished hands,
but can't return this promised land.

Days pushed back with faded years;
I've found that they still find my tears,
for men and lovers never know the
child that hides my aching heart so
help me if you think you can,
I've got to find my promised land.

The sinking sun on summer lawns;
the sight, the smell, the taste is gone.
still, nothing has been rearranged,
it's just the little girl that's changed,
and just a single golden strand that
binds her to this promised land.

I only wish I could have known
how much it hurts to find you've grown.
there's something there that says it's wrong to
weave the chains that reach so long they
tell me it's a worthless plan . . .
I'll never find that promised land.

May 28

I tutored in algebra this afternoon. Did alright. Roy sat in on AA. I walked to the lake to watch the moon rise.

May 30

How ironic it seems . . . that the pathway to my presence is blocked, guarded, by an opened window. No white light could ever strike me as I dream it would, some windy night. Never catch me blowing slightly, in my black robe . . . witch deep child remembering the early morning moon.

June 3

Child trips on over wet land, the rain playing with a chant that is uttered deep beneath the earth, and only she can hear it. The midnight blue darkness dances and taunts in splashes through the trees and catches her crystaled laughter. Only she understands it. Alone, she waits for her lover. The stallion beside her is cast bronze in the early morning moon. His mane whipping golden fingers to the wind . . . and soon the eastern stars lighten with fire, summon the day, she is gone . . . her laughter still pierces the air . . . stallion horse shudders the earth as he flees . . . only that one of Astaroth will know that she came. Blessed be. Blessed be the empty night that killed her.

I see
life here that blows like
thick steam from leaves;
we breathe leaves.
I feel
pulsing that pumps like
river rapids from mountains;
we live rivers.
I touch
darkness whose silence is like
night;
we die Night.

June 7

My pizza shop closed down. Last night was my last night there. Everyone was getting zoned but me. All the responsibility was dumped on my shoulders. I felt lonely and left out and too fucking real.

Wednesday, June 11

It rained all day. My dentist appointment proved no cavities. I went to Reachout, then hitched home to tutor. I went to AA and got my 3 month sobriety medallion.

June 15

help me, please love me,
no please stay away
for you scare me when I see
how much that you care.
why do you wait and tell me
how much that you'll miss me
when I leave for summer
and god, I'll be lonely,
but no . . .
I can manage,
you needn't be there . . .

just to touch me
I tremble and cry deep inside
for the pain
that you bring with your love
will not die . . . but my heart aches for comfort
and you can't be here
and the night chills my body and freezes my tears . . .
Now I stop and I call you,
but there where you were
there is nothing but silence
that hurts more than night
and the fright of your love when I find it was ours . . .
help me, please, love me, no . . . please find a way . . .
and be here when
night kills the lingering day . . .

Hopeless romance, here we go again.

All is dark save for silver splashes of
moonlight against your face,
dancing quietly across my eyes . . .
The silence is heavy, the message
I know, as you do,
it scares me
No one but the stars to hear the words
that might be whispered behind my pain,
and smoothing its cruel edges,
jagged, unfinished woman,
I sink back, give in
to your comforting arms,
Keeping me safe like a shell in a wave
from the realness of my thoughts
And held there, gently, I can no longer remember
why it seemed so very wrong
to be with you
My doubt is pumped like the weight of
my heart, away from my sight . . .
building a wall so high,
I can no longer see you as you are
without receding into the person that I was
before I met you.

June 24

This is my first afternoon up at camp again. Seiche cut his foot to hell. I seem to be settled in up here, but I haven't even been to lower camp yet. The days go so slowly here. I'm scared of captivity again. I don't want to face myself in such a small place for so long a time.

It's different tonight.
I can think clearly; I'm aware of my mind.
and like tonight I wish I didn't have to feel at all.
In the corner again; alone.
Music drifting from the stairwell; closer to me than anyone here.
Flashes of the way I was; the lightning paints the horses milling,
restless in the storm . . .
Alone again, frozen in a still life; unmoving.
Where I've been scares me too much to go back; and I don't know where I'm going.
And times like tonight when I wish I could hide, I am standing in a clearing.
When I wish I didn't have to feel so much like a little girl with nowhere to go . . .
there is no one here to hold me,
and tell me everything's alright . . .

June 26

It's Seiche's birthday today. The sun is just setting now. His is, too. He seems so much older all of a sudden. He can't be only nine. I went and walked in the pasture and I sat down to write a poem. Heidi the donkey came for my company. She's always apart from the others. Maybe she feels different. Maybe she's just lonely. She's a lot like me. I wrote Seiche a song. It tears my heart to see him looking so old.

To A Flame

In the morning field of wading grass; in some forgotten night
There was born a fine young stallion; stood before the morning light . . .
Still I only can imagine, since these days have long gone by . . .
how his mane blew flaxen fingers . . . and the fire danced in his eyes.
In my dreams he'll always be there; in that field that drinks the sun,
The forgotten night that left him where his days are never done.
But the time has slowed the fire, seems that nothing's quite the same,
And I damn the day before him that at last puts out the flame.
Through the path of well-worn summers, left behind with all the years,
He would take me to the moon and back and dry my lonely tears.
We were never two together, nor are one when we're apart,
It would take me all my life to find a horse with half his heart.
Now the fields are ever waiting, everytime he passes by . . .
I can hear them call him back and I can see his longing eye . . .
Where the fire still burns brightly, that will house a dying flame . . .
They will keep him there forever, in the morning fields again . . .

June 28

Dear Family,

How do you dig my stationary? It's what I dug out of my cupboards before I left. I feel guilty that I haven't written you for so long, but I know that once you know why you'll be happy. It's really odd. I'm taking this summer as a challenge. I decided that since school is something of a challenge and that since there are plenty of things I won't want to do there, that I'd better make a practice out of doing things that I don't want to do here. (Such as doing something even if I'm too sad, too tired, or if I have a headache); those were last year's excuses for hiding from myself. So far, things are going well. And usually, I end up liking the activities that I don't want to go to at first. Cinnabar, the colt, is doing very well. We decided that he's too young to drive, so I may teach Seiche instead to earn my Horsemanship. I've even been getting everywhere on time, which is a first for me. Miss Heleam seems pleased with me. I shortened the colt's mane and it makes him look like a perfect little hunter.

Well, I'm slowly overcoming my fear of sailing, in fact I rather get a thrill out of controlling the boat with the wind and heeling at such an angle that you have to lean back just to keep from falling into the lake. Or if you're working the jib, being dragged waist-deep through the water on the low side when it catches a wind-squall. In dance, I'm doing a solo to my favorite song, and another dance with some friends that's kind of silly. We're also doing some neat songs in Chorus. Well, like you said . . . keep letters "short and sweet." I must boogie.

Love,
Pony

July 20

Home again. I tripped on the trail at camp and broke my wrist, but somehow it seemed alright. I did more up there than I've ever done before. I danced, I sang, I rode (and rode), I wrote, I painted, I sailed . . . I lived again. Did everything to make use of my long-tarnished senses. That's what it feels like to be alive. It's not that way all the time, though. I realize that. Seiche is lame.

July 28

Now I'm up at this Christian camp and I'm just about to lose my mind. I just get home and I'm off for somewhere new. I knew that I wouldn't be able to go all out up here because of this damned cast. But inside I thought I might have some fun out of it anyway. I don't like to feel singled out. I want to be freer to do more things.

July 30

Sue left to go up to her cabin today. It seems like just lately we've been missing each other wherever we go. I get back from camp and she leaves, then I go somewhere else and she comes home. Today she had to say goodbye to her horse, Casey. I guess she's moving somewhere and can't keep him. God, it was sad. We rode together this morning and returned home around 2:00. I really didn't realize that that was her last ride on him . . . When her mother came by to take her, we walked out to the barn together. Then it hit me. She walked around to his stall. "Goodbye, baby . . . yes . . . Goodbye Casey. I love you . . . " her voice broke. "Listen . . . you take good care of these people, o.k.? You be good.

Bye. I love you . . ."

I walked out ahead of her so that she could be alone for a moment. She followed soon after and we walked in silence toward the car. Then she turned and broke down. I gave her a good strong hug. It seemed like forever; both of us crying and saying our thankyou's and goodbye's through the tears. "I love you, too . . . " she said. I couldn't see her face when the car drove down the driveway. "Take care . . . " I whispered after her. "I'll miss you . . . "

August 1

I feel like giving up. It's a constant, killing battle to live and stay real, too. The thing is, I am unhappy being straight. I don't want to be the way I am. I guess I never have. Everyone, or almost everyone here seems to have an escape for whenever they need it. *Jesus.* I don't understand. I'm so screwed up. I've been an off and on Christian for too long. I don't know what to believe because I've heard too much. From being on both sides. I almost hate Christians and I don't know why. I want help and I need the support, but damn it, I don't understand. What is right? These people here have something I don't, and I have an empty space inside. I can feel it. They say Jesus did this and that. How can they know that? I need something so desperately. I'm really, really scared. Those fucking cold winters that ice over my soul and kill me. I'm alone again and facing school. I don't think I'm going to make it. I feel weak and suseptable to anything. Open to attack. Maybe I've never thought I could make it. All this time I've just been waiting to die. Part of me says fight on, and the rest of me says fuck everything. Give up. Stay sick. I want to live if I can be happy part of the time, but if my life is so much a constant, tearing struggle to keep my head above the water, I might as well drop and let myself sink.

Back from nothingness
to a place where the world tastes of every tree
and cloud in a strange, sweet breath of summer
I see with my tongue how blue the sky is
and taste with my eyes all that is there
But the nothingness that prevails beneath my senses
will not die when I close my eyes . . .

Any other plan but hers seems to follow through
and every other song she hears seems to come back to you.
When the frost killed the field, she remembered how it died
where she knelt in the snow, felt the white turn black inside
and the days all ran together and the nights were all she knew
of the searching, silent midnights; of the lonliness that grew.
With every hour her nightmares deepened, til her thoughts were near
insane
She could never make it fast enough to quite outrun the pain.

I don't understand you, you are there . . . or are you?
What are you?Who are you?What do you want of me?You love me and
if you're there I won't let you in.I am scared of you.What will you
do with me?

August 5

Tutoring once again takes over the week. Tomorrow, four, maybe five hours of cramming to finish a chapter. Tom came home from summer school. All too old, it seems. The horses are doing alright. I'm in that same rotten place where I'm lonely as hell even when I'm with people. It's winter in my gut and I've already lost. Those damned doors keep calling me back.

Late last night I thought I saw Joella.

The more I'm gone from there
The harder he searches where
I've been for where I am
but I'm not there. I am
staying more away from where he thinks I am or should be soon
but now he's learned to pass me by when I am there where I should be
I am here when he goes.

Dear Pony,

How did the rest of camp go for you? I should hope well. I was really bummed out to find out that you were going to be coming home a week after I left because I really wanted to see you. You are such a big part of my life that your absence is really wierd. The girl I drove out west with has no "child" whatsoever, but is always yelling at me because I act like such a kid. I guess I don't like acting grown up all the time because you have to be so serious. I really miss your laughter and the good hugs you gave me. I can't believe that it won't be until Christmas that I see you again. So many changes will have happened by then . . . Thank God our friendship won't change.

It's almost easier staying straight out here because no one knows me and they don't know my past. It scares me because everyone thinks I have my head on so straight. They say they want to learn from me and that makes me really nervous. I feel good about myself but I wish I had you to talk to to share my ideas with and to help each other out when it gets hard.

Lots of Love,
Sue

The 6th

What matters? The unsaid things within do. They tell me how alive the Speed Queen is. I wrote a long time ago . . . "look forward to summer, but dread the horror of another cold and lonely winter. Another day . . ."

I have the time to run away from all my past has been,
I fought the battle, fell down hard, and stood back up again.
And for them I have no answers, they will have to find their own . . .
if they have the guts to do it, then they'll have to come alone.

August 12

Inside I know that to get into riding and showing more, I must also get a better horse. Seiche has been so patient and loving. When I sell him, I'll be selling most of my past. So many things he's been around for. He was around for the hardest part of my growing up. He helped me grow up. I love him, but it's time to move on. It's all in growing. Losing and gaining. Things must change to grow. That's why everything must change. It's all beginning to make sense.

As long as I still believe in what I say, I shall be sane enough.
As long as my feet walk straight by the road, I shall think clearly enough.
As long as justice is done to my judgements, I shall be truthful enough.
As long as darkness is my master, I shall be . . .

Sept. 17

No, I am not screwed up. Seiche's hurting and I'm too scared to even go outside to feed him. What's out there that scares me so?

Sept. 19

I got my license yesterday. Met with the group back on the

road. Kevin found us out. Oh my fucking head. I think I'm going to be sick.

Sept. 20

31 minutes until Equinox. I passed them several times tonight. No change in the atmosphere. You can run, but you just can't hide. This time last year it was a Friday game at Clairdale. Once round the full moon cycle. Blessed Equinox. The Fall Solstice comes again. Only to be bled in full as the moon. Ten minutes. Help. Ten lousy minutes and the whole big dark damned world comes down and sinks another foot into the earth.

To Claire . . . the one that didn't come home . . .

Rain on the lake sinks a part of me with every raindrop.
down under the wavey blue, the water's calm and keeps me
safe from the storm . . .
Rocks me softly in her mothering arms
as I become a child of the lake; a sister to the deep and green . . .
far and quiet from the raging storm.
I close my eyes and surrender
to her gentle lullaby and sink; I feel the slow and falling spiral
to the mother's sandy womb; sunk with every raindrop
through the deep and green . . .
and silent.

Sept. 22

Seiche did very well at the show. He picked up a high point trophy. Cinnabar Foxe was alright, I just wish he wasn't so rowdy. Some friend of Mom's told her he thought I'd grown up so . . .

Sept. 23

I drove to school. I actually wore a dress for once. Jerry Martin killed himself. All of the kids from the halfway house went to his visitation. They were all scared. It could have been any of us. I'll never forget the lines of kids, all standing together like an army around him; arms around each other . . . silent.

Sept 24

Try and live without and you desire what you never realized you had before to come back. To stand by you, to talk with . . . to stay warm . . . and suddenly there is nothing.

Sept. 28

Roy had just passed me when I approached the corner. The light was green. I signaled, looked, and started my turn. Suddenly there was this car coming at me going like a bat out of hell. The brakes screeched and I shut my eyes as the metal crunched and the car shifted violently on two wheels. I was snapped sideways when the car came down and banged my head against the windshield. I drifted to the curb.

I felt the air on my face; my recorder booming "Stairway to Heaven" full blast. I heard people. I flew back and lodged myself in the past. My life was flying out from under me.

There was the voice of my counselor in Detox. "I haven't seen her for months and all of a sudden I see her like this." I couldn't make my voice work. I couldn't move. Then I heard Roy and someone grabbed my wrist to find a pulse. Someone was holding my head and neck in traction.

"Out cold," someone else said. "I can't get a reaction."

"Is she breathing?" Red lights swam around my head and drew me in slowly in a sickening pool of death. "The ambulance should be here any minute."

"Who called it? . . . "

"What's her name?"

"Joan."

"Joan, does your back hurt?" The black pressed in closer.

"Joan, Joan . . . "

"Here's the ambulance . . . " The air was cold. There was a light in my eyes.

"Here, I can wake her . . . she knows me . . . " It was Roy's voice. There was a hand on my neck. "Joan . . . wake up . . . C'mon . . . "

"Let's get her out of here. Out of sight anyway." Suddenly there was nothing under me. I hit something soft and they zipped a blanket over me.

"I think she can hear us."

"She's coming around."

I was in a field. The lights on my car were out. The tape was playing "Stairway to Heaven" really slowly, as the batteries died. I had no movement. There were no cars there anymore. The huge man-goat creature was gone from sight. There was a heavy stench like dirty straw around me. Something tapped on my rear window and I shifted my eyes . . .

"Joan, Joan . . . can you hear us?" I was staring at an oxygen mask on a white expanse of ceiling. "Her parents are here," Roy said. The darkness took me over.

Oct. 2

In for physical therapy. Went to a few classes. My back is really sore. It hurts, but there is nothing for it. They gave me Valiums and Tylenol with codiene. I couldn't take them, of course. I hate being chemically dependant sometimes. It doesn't seem fair that I just sit here and hurt and I can do nothing for it.

Oct. 3

The house waits for me. That old abandoned house; it almost owns me . . . Yes, it owns me. Be all of the world, and none of the dark. The legions of fallen ones come quickly, "Hark!" The powers of earth, the powers of hell . . . we call to us one who has broken the spell. We knock at her door; we chill her good mind . . . her heart shall beat swiftly, her eyes be but blind. The flames will posess her within Satan's breath. Be damned unto Satan, we bind thee til death! So mote it be.

Oct. 5

To Jesus people church with Kevin and family. What a night.

Tues., Oct. 7

Windy and wild. Leaves whipped my body as I walked. The song is the same, the words have been changed. The "Silas" house is infested. She will be safe.

Oct. 12

Fixed the fence, cleaned the barn. The blood of Jesus Christ is long ago dried up. I feel hopeless. Why aren't we free?

Mon., Oct. 13

Out of money. Believe me, it shows. Dark house, no gas, no more horse feed. Tell that to the stupid fly that won't leave me alone . . .

> Early morning moon come land on my shoulder
> lightly, let me know that you're still there.
> Shine a dark blueness in the sky . . . That sees my teardrop
> glistening . . . the only thing that moves, save the trees
> falls along my cheek and splashes in brilliant night
> colors that the moon catches . . . and tosses to the stars . . .

Told the Silas house goodnight and my high beams folded in the earth and tucked it in for the night. Baby, I wanna stand by you . . . Hide in your darkness. Your eyes are so deep and dark like the empty, old orphan you are . . . You stand crying. The cars rush on by. I see your tears.

Tuesday, Oct. 14

I'm in the cafeteria taking a stupid test. Bell rang, gotta go again. By the time I'm twenty, it seems I'll have more written on me than Jesus ever did. I wonder how fast the rest of the day will go? Hallomas is coming.

> Silas, blessed Silas, 'tween they fallen eaves we linger.
> Something powerful within thee holds us close within thy doors . . .
> In thy darkness, you will light us.
> By thy sheltered walls we worship,
> something silent in your comfort
> 'tween the ceiling and the floors . . .

Oct. 17

Last night my favorite place in the world burned to the ground. So everything changes . . . no one hurt. Oh, really?

What I said at the house still stands. I could change a few words now, but it's all there. Everything but the house. Scrawled in ink on a wet board. "Sometimes I wonder if I'm ever gonna make it home again . . . " And upon exploring the singed and smoking lower floor, I found it again. It smelled of all the horrors of the fire. The hot, charred pine wood, drenched with water and smeared with ashes . . . What's left of my life depends on that house. Its ruins are mine. Its memories will not leave. (I am wounded and dangerous.)

I love that Silas. I don't know why. I would not be the one to close the coffin lid of a dear friend. It drags on me and saps my energy while it stands on one leg, dripping blood from its walls. Exposed pipes and wiring protruding from the blackened rubble like bones and veins. The life drains from it. I stand by it, taking all that will leave, and giving them a home. My hand rests on the wounds of Silas, watching its every breath, knowing soon that one will be the last. Thinking that, at least, but still it holds on . . . refusing to let go and lose the fight. Only Silas and I know how much has been lost.

To the House

They tell me it's abandoned, and that,
"Good news, no one's hurt,"
as the flames explode inside themselves
and fling the settled dirt . . .
Where before it went unoticed
spiraled red into the sky,
and the crowds I thought would save you;
they just came to watch you die.
Silas, blessed Silas,
feel my aching heart for thee
Still you tremble eaves of battle scars
that's what they want to see;
See your aged foundation falter
with the agonizing flames
Eat away thy gentle spirit,
leaving you and I to blame.
For only I could know you
on a night without a moon,
when the stars would drench your windows,
come and splash into my room.
For nothing's left for anyone,
but nothing has been lost . . .
they feared your silent power
so they made you pay the cost.
Spinning, whirling, feel like dancing . . .
tearing down thy bloody walls . . .
For thy power will not dwindle
when the final ceiling falls . . .
Let them laugh and think you dead . . .
for soon those painful scars will leave,
then Silas, blessed Silas . . .
if they only could believe . . .

Tues., Nov. 4

I'm in the library, but I'm not high. Sitting in the same desk, but I know I'm all here. This time in my life is just like a cloud passing over and it won't stay. It's one of those ridiculous phases of growing up.

One more time, I am sitting in a different state of mind
cursing flies that land and (brush) and land on
morning candy bars crushed and crumbled wrappers eat the
daylight studyhall as various losers and one or two
winners mill listlessly about the ping pong nets and watch
the clock move on . . .

Nov. 10

I'm going out with Mark for the fourth time. I got my CB radio installed. The blacksmith came and did the horses. Mark and I watched TV all day.

Nov. 13

I slept out in the field last night. It snowed. My clothes got frozen so I became an early morning streaker to the house. I missed AA. Know something? I think I'm gonna be alright. At peace, finally. Finally worth it. Worth everything.

Sat., Nov. 16

Saw Mark briefly. I threw an egg at Kevin.

Mon. Nov. 19

Mark and I went to Blue Valley Rifle Range to shoot. My arm is stiff. I think I hit the target once.

Sun., Nov. 25

Found Mark and we rode Seiche and Casey up to Country Kitchen. Casey got loose. It was cold out, but it felt good.

Tuesday, Nov. 27

I have a fantastic story to tell, but my pen just got rigor mortis. That's better (new pen). I found this dog frozen outside school. I led him home with my purse strap and called him Rusty. He looked like a Rusty. I searched the Lost and Founds and there was this ad for a dog, lost, that answered to Rusty. It was him. He was a far out dog. The little boy had tears in his eyes when he saw him. Wow. That feels great. I got a job at Country Kitchen.

Thursday, Dec. 11

I returned from the hospital yesterday. I hit my head and had a touch of amnesia. It was strange having no identity. I was scared to be no one so I became another girl. I even had another name. I had to be someone. Things came back slowly. The car accident, the fire . . . too much to remember in so short a time. I must have been moving a bit too fast. It's time to slow down and look at myself.

Dec. 13

I was given an owl last night. His name was Joel; now it's Damien. He's winking awake by my bed at the moment. He's a mean little sucker. He eats too many rats and crawly stuff . . . eating me out of attic and cellar. Soon get rid of him when his purpose has been fulfilled.

Good-bye

Few words passed are understood
and silence leaves company to break down to tears.
The pain blurs her head and she stumbles and strokes
the shaggy head of the horse . . .
The hurt closes the gate and locks it tight,
but all things must change and nothing stays the same . . .
it opens still,
and she throws herself against his body . . .
massive, comforting, as it has been
so many times before.
The tears come and mat his fur against her face.
With closed eyes she looses all ropes,
and he waits . . .
The herd is running in the foggy distance;
she cries out for her love . . . she sees the longing in his eye.
The freedom reflected on the crystal surface erases all
memories of past summers,
and cool evening lakes that drink the sun,
and dusty roads that stretch on.
She falls as he moves from her and trots to the hill . . .
He pauses and looks back . . . (I love you)
(I love you, too, baby, . . . Good-bye)
and the dashing herd picks him off as it passes his way
and she stands . . . the field blurs to an antique gold . . .
Not a soul in sight . . .
but the resounding thunder of hooves
against the barren earth echoes in her head . . .
and wafts into a
dark and silent
lullaby.

Dec. 26

Jan. 4

How do you like that? This diary has actually missed both Merry Christmas and a Happy New Year. I could say "Merry Christmas and all that," like I have before . . . and I could say, "Happy New Year, nothing's changed." Gosh, even last year I admitted things had changed. For the worse, I'm afraid.

But now . . . Now! I'm on my way; I know I am. I broke up with Mark. But that was alright. I know it was the right thing to do. He told me he loved me but I couldn't find the same feeling for him. I still can't quite touch what love is. Maybe it was there, but if it wasn't, well, . . . I didn't want to hurt him. Unfortunately, I think I did. No way around it. Don't know what you got til it's gone.

Jan. 14

And I looked at my watch at a quite appropriate time
'cause my head was getting burdened with the love I could not find
so I set the hands ahead a few and dropped it at his feet
and he said those same damn words I told him never to repeat
so I pointed out the second hand and told him it was late
and he said he understood, but still he told me he would wait.
And it made me suffer more to hear him say he'd be my friend
when all I really wanted was for all of it to end . . .
then the watch was hurled into a field amidst the waist-high grass
and I lay beneath the winter sun and saw it turn to brass.
When I woke, my room was empty, and the snow had left the ground
I know not yet which was the dream . . . the watch has not been found.

Jan. 22

To hell with lonely sleeping bags. To hell with gas money, school. Behind again, as usual . . . what a drag, you're a scag . . . you lonely rag.

I am not unique
but I'm tired of being friends with a
gaggle storm of flies the more
I reach for them the more they think I'm "off" and
they get buzzed but
my old wings have been stilled . . .
someone said that I'd been killed,
but I'm here . . .
I am not scared
but I'm in the dark with people that do
not know where to go the more
I follow them the more they think I'm hunting;
they get haunted but
my old ghost has been crystalized and
I can see him in their eyes
it tells me
I am here.

Tuesday, Jan. 27

Time passes so quickly. A month folds into a year and the year turns around. Friday I will have been sober for one year. Tonight I went to a meeting at Brent's on chemical dependency and activities we could have for recovering addicts.

Mom is deep into a half-way house committee. Dad is filming commercials in Montreal. Tom is on Cozumel Island in Mexico for a school trip. I'm right here. In pain. That's right. Being real isn't all a circus. It hurts sometimes, too. That's the only thing that makes it real. That's the only thing that helps you grow.

Tomorrow I may not own Seiche anymore. Things must change . . . But it's painful. Six years is a long amount of memories. And for probably the most important years of my life, he was always there. Even when I wasn't. I love him so much. I could keep him, but nobody lives in a fairy tale childhood forever. Not this kid, anyway. Break away . . . move on . . . accept the hurt and go from there.

January 29

Funny how important things always happen on January 30th. Senor Thunder's registration papers will be handed to me tomorrow and he will be mine. A new horse. Just like a new start. Faithful Seiche is off to the good life in Maple Brook. Cinnabar is growing like a weed, and all around me . . . everything is changing. Tomorrow is the day I hit St. Vincent's one year ago.

I remember the freezing cold that made the snow crunch like hard styrofoam beneath my feet. I remember so many things. I guess I should be thankful for what this one year has given me. I AM thankful. It was the year that I was born, in a sense. I'm still learning how to love people. There are no more plastic friends telling me that "it's alright" when I'm half dead. Those people still exist, but they don't tell anyone much of anything anymore. I'm living — who used to only exist, and did so quite nearly to death. There wasn't a time or a situation that didn't teach me something. I have a long way to go, but I've come so far already . . .

I woke up this morning with a restless, impending feeling of duty before me. I held back my tears all day. Now I'm alone with my thoughts. The radio is endlessly chattering by my bed, a pot of dead flowers stare blankly at the wall . . . and a small lead horse grazes intently on my alarm clock. Alone with my thoughts. Now Seiche is gone.

When I walk in the barn I see a promising young colt. But before him I see senseless nametags over nails, under saddles . . . The names of a horse that no one else could know the way I have. The name of his friend that broke his leg. The cobwebs seem so much darker over these than ever before. The emptiness of the place is screaming at me. Six years gone in one day.

It was a long, lonely ride to his final home. I laughed as I always had at the trucks that honked and the drivers that tried to scare him. I think he thought we were just riding until we came to the highway. Then his pace slowed and his feet dragged. The lines around his eyes deepened. He sensed it. A train passed us in Long Lake and he stopped and looked up at it; contemplating. I wrote our song.

I see a train comin . . . there ain't no tracks
I got a feelin that I won't be comin back.
There may be sunshine and there may be rain . . . Be a long time before it breaks in through the pain.
I'm hearing whistles from a non-existant train . . .

I led him up the last road and stopped at the end. I knew I couldn't say good-bye to him at the farm. This is it, I thought. He was staring across the fields.

I threw my arms around his neck and hung there for a moment. I quietly thanked him for his life. Then I sang him a song.

Today, while the blossoms still cling to the vine
I'll taste your strawberries, I'll drink your sweet wine
A million tomorrows shall all pass away . . .
e'er I forget all the joys that are mine . . . today . . .
["Today" by Randy Sparks]

If I can ever forget the warm summer afternoons at the farm . . . being so happy just to be with him, learning what loneliness is and facing alienation; if I can forget the many times he saved me from going one step too close to death with drugs, the windyblue nights of stargazing, the red lights racing across their steaming bodies in the early morning, the challenges, the defeats, the tears, the joy, the swimming in the lake . . . if I can forget the longest, hardest ride I've ever had to make, the passing miles tearing away at my heart as they will forever . . . then I'd be forgetting the most fantastic, patient and gentle creature that God ever laid down on this green earth.

The final stretch of that ride did not mark the end of anything for me. Rather; it was a kind of victory. The little horse made of lead that I bought the day Seiche became mine is still here. But his empty stall stands. His bridle that I made in treatment with his name across the browband is covered with cobwebs. It will never be slipped over his head again.

In spite of this grief, I must realize that he will be happy with his friends now, and that I should be grateful for the joy he brought me during the darkest years of my life.

Halfway from the hell, he's brought me
Love to fill my heart, he's taught me
Can't forget . . . no, I'll never forget
the nights he's pulled me through . . .
They've been the darkest nights I've
ever had the will to fight I've
got to get movin, but he's got to know I love him, too.
Halfway from the home I gave him
hoping somehow I could save him

can't forget . . . no, I musn't forget
my life is changing, too . . .
They say you can't hold on to dreams forever
let them fly before they sever
Give them wings to do what they must do . . .
It seems the longest ride I've ever had, so much to hide
I've never known why; never knew that dream would be you . . .
Halfway to a distant home . . . he left, I left;
we're left alone.
Unpaid for all the hell you've brought me through
includes that lonely road that leads from you . . .
but damn, old friend, you know I love you, too . . .
To one hell of a horse, and my best friend.

Friday, January 29

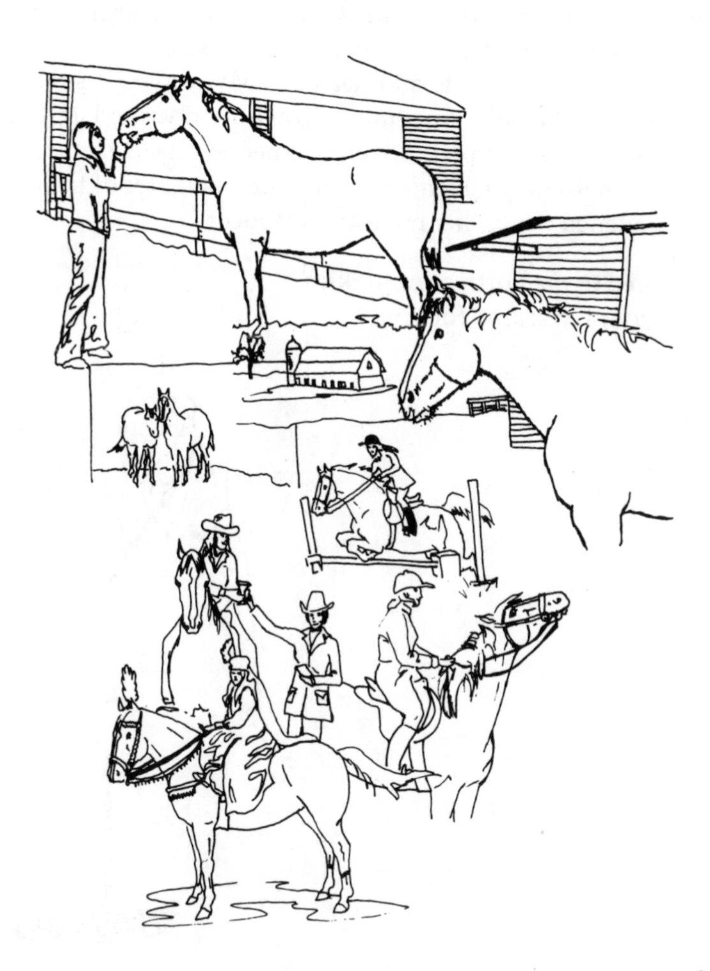

January 30

So I made it. Today I made it. This isn't really the end or the beginning of anything special, but today I have been straight for one year. I am alive, and I can feel myself growing. Someone, I think Kevin, told me once that a muscle isn't building itself until it starts hurting. That's the same for being real. It doesn't always hurt, but it seems that twards the end of this diary I only entered something in it when I was feeling hurt. Believe me, there have been good times. Like the times spent just talking with good friends, the rowdy-but-once-again innocent nights in Willowood . . . and there were the angry times, like having nothing for the pain of a back injury because of my dependency, and there were the in between times, the happy and hurting and scared times . . . like the first time I put my arms around my mother, and my father . . . and my dear brother.

Tomorrow, finally, is another day. My prayer is simple: that tears be the only thing my sorrows are drowned in, that my happiness might paint love in someone's heart sometime . . . and that I may never forget the frigid laughter of the one with leadened wings; her majesty the Queen.

Dedicated to the north door junkies;
I love you; I'm scared for you.

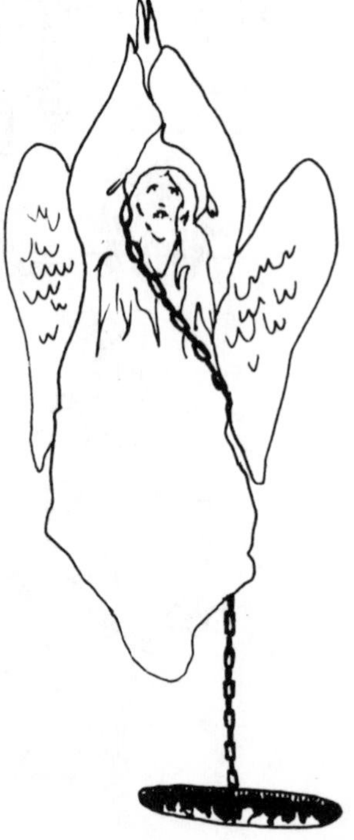

P.S. . . It's not alright.

Epilogue: A Poem

I am sorry for the silence
  that grew with changing years
  for the times I hid my heartbreak
  at your lost and lonely tears.
  Now my thoughts weave spotless cobwebs —
      and I watch my old self die.
 Please remember,
      you were once
   as young and scared as I.